Berlitz

Thailand

Front cover: Wat Phra That Doi Suthep

Right: The orchid, Thailand's favourite flower

TOP 10 ATTRACTIONS

Kwai River Bridge • Pay homage to the thousands of prisoners who died during the bridge's construction in World War II *(page 38)*

Mae Hong Son • Long a destination for those seeking old-world serenity, this northeastern town lies in a beautiful forested valley *(page 70)*

Bangkok's Wat Phra Kaew and Grand Palace complex • Highlights include the chapel of the Emerald Buddha and a golden *chedi* (stupa) *(page 26)*

Chiang Mai • For Thai silks visit the bustling Night Bazaar *(page 61)*

Phang Nga Bay • Paddle around a landscape filled with oddly shaped islands and hidden caves *(page 76)*

Phanom Rung • This spectacular sanctuary is one of the highlights of the Khmer Culture Trail *(page 17)*

Ayutthaya • A national treasure, this ruined city gives an insight into the ancient history of Thailand *(page 41)*

Hill tribes • Trek by Jeep or on foot to see these followers of ancient rituals *(page 64)*

Ko Samui • The place to swim, snorkel, windsurf, dine on the sand or just people-watch *(page 78)*

Chao Phraya • Take a boat on Bangkok's majestic river *(page 35)*

CONTENTS

23

82

93

66

90
38

INTRODUCTION

As the only country in Southeast Asia that was never colonised, Thailand explodes with the boundless energy and self-confidence of its people. Literally translated, Thailand means 'Land of the Free', although it is most often referred to as 'Land of Smiles'. The Thais are easy-going, content and proud of their country. And they are always smiling. They value *jai yen* or a 'cool heart' and dislike hot tempers and loud voices. They are warm and welcoming to foreigners. Even on Bangkok's impossibly crowded streets, a visitor will feel quite safe asking a stranger for directions. There is a sense of peace and tolerance that prevails throughout the country, perhaps due to the fact that over 90 percent of the population is Buddhist.

Buddhism is central to the Thai way of life

Founded in India, Buddhism first came to Thailand in 3BC, when it thrived as the religion of kings and as a unifier of the people. Shrines, Buddha replicas and temples are found in abundance in every city and village. The Buddhist philosophy permeates all facets of national life. Wherever you go, you will see monks with orange robes and shaven heads strolling the streets. Visit a temple and you may even witness an ordination ceremony when saffron-robed novices are carried high above the shoulders of their friends and families.

Long-tail boats at Ko Phi Phi

Thailand and Its Attractions

Roughly the size of Texas or France, Thailand offers a vast variety of holiday possibilities. You'll find thick jungles, bustling cities and sparkling beach resorts. In the northern city of Chiang Mai, you'll find one of the world's most fascinating night markets. Those interested in purchasing silk, woven baskets and lacquered wood will want to shop here; it's also an excellent place to purchase imitation designer-wear at incredibly low prices. In the lush valleys north of Chiang Mai you'll find the many orchid farms and elephant training camps that give Thailand its unique identity.

Rice fields and jungle near Chiang Rai

Going deeper into the northern regions, to Chiang Rai and the Golden Triangle, you'll find hill-tribes following rituals established thousands of years ago. Don't miss the opportunity to take a boat-trip down the Mekong, one of the world's great rivers. It runs down from Tibet, irrigating the rice fields in the north of Thailand before it empties out in the Mekong Delta of South Vietnam. If it's trekking into the jungles that you're after, then head further northwest, to the town of Mae Hong Son, deep in the jungle bordering Myanmar (Burma), where jeep tours and overnight camping trips can be arranged.

In the centre of the country there are tranquil rice fields stretching as far as the eye can see, and the magnificent ruins of Sukhothai and Ayutthaya. If you prefer more natural attractions, head for one of the vast national parks, which now constitute a huge 34,500 sq km (23,479 sq miles) portion of Thailand. Of particular note is Khao Yai National Park where iridescent kingfishers and orange-breasted, red-headed trogons flit beneath the shade of the leafy canopy. Gibbons and flying squirrels, elephants, black bears and tigers dwell in these vast stretches of dense evergreen. You might catch a glimpse of any one of over 900 different species. Orchids grow in abundance, and there is a multitude of butterflies.

Thai customs

On being introduced, Thais will place both palms of their hands together under their chin in a traditional Wai greeting. The head is considered sacred in Buddhism; try not to touch anyone, even children, there.

And in the south, in the Gulf of Thailand, and off the sandy shores of the Andaman Sea you'll find spectacular tropical islands jutting out of the shimmering blue water. The resorts of Phuket, Ko Phi Phi and Ko Samui attract sunworshippers from around the world. Here, the beach is the main attraction and there are many world-class hotels and resorts to suit every taste and budget.

Many visitors begin their visit in Bangkok where direct flights from around the world arrive at the Bangkok International Airport. Thailand's capital is one of the most crowded cities in Asia. It has the majestic River of the Kings and many criss-crossing canals. The old way of life still exists along the waterways and the floating market is still a sight to behold, but these days you are more likely to find endless traffic jams and scores of high-rise buildings. After the initial shock of Bangkok's polluted and chaotic streets, you will

The Phra Si Rattana Chedi at Wat Phra Kaew in Bangkok

begin to discover the city's many splendid sights. From the glorious Temple of Dawn to the magnificent reclining Buddha and the impressive Grand Palace, Bangkok is rich in royal, religious and historical monuments. It has excellent shopping in its many malls and endless shop-lined streets.

With its diverse range of restaurants, the city is also a food-lover's paradise. Fresh, delicious and inexpensive food is found practically everywhere in this city of more than 10 million residents. Given the simple street-side eateries to elegant dining rooms overlooking the Chao Phraya river, you will definitely eat well in Bangkok. Thai cooking is based on dividing foods into spicy, sour, hot and sweet; and the success of any meal relies on creating delightful contrasts, which ensure that the palate never becomes jaded. Popular delicacies such as prawns in coconut, or succulent chicken wrapped in a banana leaf take their place among an array of hotter culinary specialities. It would probably be possible to enjoy a different type of dish every day of your visit and leave with plenty of fine dishes still unsampled.

When to Go

To some visitors, the climate can seem even more novel than the food. Thailand's weather is classified as hot, hotter and hottest. The hottest months are March to May when the country is at its driest before the rains arrive. June to October is the less hot monsoon season, when the rains come in heavy downpours, usually in the afternoons, but only lasting for an hour or two. November to February is the least hot period and inevitably forms the high tourist season in Thailand. Cool northern winds blow down from China, which makes Bangkok slightly more tolerable for visitors.

Although many travellers avoid the country during the monsoon months, this can actually be a very pleasant time to visit. Domestic flights are virtually empty and temples and beaches are not as crowded. If you don't mind the occasional rains, then you'll be rewarded with reduced hotel rates and restaurants eager to please the adventurous off-season traveller.

Selling produce at a floating market

A Warm Welcome

In the final analysis, Thailand's people – even more than the sights, the scenery and the food – often afford the most memorable experiences. From friendly northerners who may sell you sweet honey pineapple by the side of the road to the smiling rice farmers in the central plains, the philosophy underlying every aspect of life is, simply, *mai pen rai* ('no worries').

A BRIEF HISTORY

Recent archaeological finds in northeast Thailand (formerly Siam) are turning traditional ideas on their head. Relics discovered in the village of Ban Chiang dating back over 5,000 years are still being studied, but seem to prove that Thailand was home to one of the first Bronze Age civilisations, predating that of China.

What happened to those prehistoric people is not known. As for the Thais, it is probable that they did not reach the area until the 11th or 12th century. According to anthropologists, they then spread south across vast areas of the fertile Chao Phraya valley, at the same time displacing both the Mons and Khmers. Around AD 1259, the kingdom of Lanna ('Land of a Million Rice Fields') was established in what is now northern Thailand. Chiang Rai was chosen as capital to start with, but when King Mengrai spotted five white mice, two white *sambars* (a type of elk) and two white barking deer together on the banks of the Ping River, he relocated the capital to Chiang Mai.

Khmer heritage at Phimai, central Thailand

Mengrai ruled prosperously until the age of 80, when he was struck by lightning.

Dawn of Happiness

The first great chapter of Thai history began with King Ramkamhaeng the Great, ruler of Sukhothai (founded in the 1230s) around 1280 to 1317. King Ramkamhaeng – renowned for legendary exploits on elephants – nur-

Sukhothai, centre of a once powerful kingdom

tured a powerful kingdom that was a thriving centre for the arts. In its heyday, the kingdom stretched from Lampang in the north of Thailand to Vientiane, now part of Laos, and south towards the Malay Peninsula. Sukhothai contributed some of the finest examples of Thai sculpture in history, many of which can still be viewed in parts of the old city today.

After the death of King Ramkamhaeng, the kingdom's power declined. By the 15th century the city of Sukhothai was little more than a provincial town, and shortly afterwards it was abandoned altogether.

Ayutthaya

Established in 1350, Ayutthaya continued for over 400 years and earned a place as one of the East's greatest civilisations.

Under King U-Thong and a succession of legendary monarchs, the kingdom expanded rapidly. Towards the end of the 14th century, the Khmers were driven out of vast areas

Reclining Buddha in saffron robe at Ayutthaya

of central and northern Thailand, and the people of Sukhothai were finally vanquished. In 1431 the capital at Angkor in Cambodia was sacked, and Ayutthaya's pre-eminence was established beyond question. It became a centre for trade between China, India and Europe, in which teak and spices were bartered for gold and for cannons, which the Siamese pulled behind their elephants.

In spite of the loss of several kings – who were either cudgelled to death or poisoned – the people of Ayutthaya were, by all accounts, a happy lot, 'much given to pleasure and ryot' according to the observations of one 17th-century traveller. Opium was in quite abundant supply, and cohabitation and wife-swapping found many enthusiastic supporters.

Many foreign travellers who visited Ayutthaya during the 17th century were impressed by the size and opulence of the Siamese capital. Directors of the East India Company compared it favourably with London, estimating its population to be anything from 300,000 to 1 million. With palaces, canals and temples, the city acquired a justified reputation for being the most beautiful in southeastern Asia.

European influence reached its zenith during the reign of King Narai (1656–88), when the courts of Siam were visited by ambassadors from as far away as the court of Louis XIV, along with explorers, zealous Jesuit missionaries and traders. One Greek adventurer, named Geraki Constantine Phaulkon, was even appointed the king's first minister, and acted as the principal go-between when diplomatic exchanges were held. Such apparent favouritism inevitably sparked jealousy. Shortly before the king died in 1688, at the time of a bloody revolt, Phaulkon was arrested and then executed. Following this incident, Thailand had almost no contact with the West for a period of 150 years.

Between the 15th and 18th centuries, the Thais fought innumerable battles against the neighbouring Burmese. In April 1767, the Burmese succeeded in capturing Ayutthaya, after a 14-month-long siege. They pillaged the city and vandalised every aspect of Thai culture and art. The sack of Ayutthaya, a great tragedy in Thai history, still casts a shadow over the national consciousness of the Thai people.

Absolute Rule

When it came to rhetorical flourishes, the monarchs of Ayutthaya in the 17th century took the biscuit. Any mortal who was so bold as to address the king was obliged to start as follows: 'High and mighty Lord of me, thy slave, I desire to take thy royal word and put it in my brain and on the top of my head.' Those who failed to follow this code of conduct were summarily chastised with bamboos. Others were buried alive in the cement walls surrounding the city.

One survivor, a young general from Tak province, rallied the remnants of the Thai army and managed to expel the Burmese garrison. Ayutthaya had been almost totally destroyed, however, so Taksin – as he was known – founded a new capital at Thonburi, directly across the Chao Phraya river from what has since become Bangkok. Though his father was actually Chinese – and a commoner at that – Taksin was crowned King of Thailand. He ruled until 1782, at which point he was dethroned on the grounds that he had gone mad. The life of the once-great general ended most abruptly when he was ceremoniously executed with a club of scented sandalwood.

From Thonburi to Bangkok

The death of Taksin saw the rise to power of the Chakri Dynasty, the greatest in Thai history, and the one that still occupies the throne today. Rama I, the first Chakri-dynasty

European impression of Ayutthaya in the 17th century

king, immediately moved his
capital from Thonburi to
Bangkok – on the east bank
of the river – saying that the
new city would be larger
and easier to defend. He
then went on to defeat a
number of marauding Bur-
mese expeditions.

His son, Rama II, devoted
himself to preserving Thai
literature, and produced a
classic version of the Thai
Ramakien, based on the epic
Sanskrit poem, *Ramayana*.
He also re-established rela-
tions with the West, and still

Buddha in Wat Arun, which was
built by Rama II and Rama III

found time to sire 73 children by 38 mothers.

Although no less influential, Rama III (1824–51) is largely
overlooked by historians. As a devout Buddhist he built some
of Bangkok's finest temples, including Wat Arun and parts of
Wat Pho. He also went on to introduce Western medicine to
his country – including smallpox vaccinations – as well as
arranging for American missionaries to visit the country; one
of them brought the first printing press with Thai type.

The King and I

The most renowned of the early monarchs is better known
for his excessive libido than his actual achievements. Despite
this, the Thais worship Mongkut as one of their greatest and
most progressive monarchs. Not only was he a man of some
sophistication, he was also better educated than most of his
contemporaries in Europe. It was during his reign that com-
moners were allowed for the first time to set eyes on the King

Statue of King Rama VI

of Siam. Waterways and roads were built, and laws passed to improve rights for women and children.

Mongkut was succeeded by Rama V, who became known as Chulalongkorn, or Lord of the White Elephant, and was one of the most popular and enlightened of the Chakri kings. During his 42-year reign, he abolished slavery and established a schooling system, the first post office and a national library. He led his country literally as well as symbolically into the 20th century, and is remembered with considerable affection today.

The World Wars

The effect of World War I was to propel Thailand out of isolation. In 1918, King Vajiravudh (Rama VI) dispatched troops to France to support the Allied cause. A likely explanation for his sympathies is that he was Cambridge-educated and had served for a time in the British army. Once the war was over, Siam became a member of the League of Nations.

One legacy of Rama VI was the use of surnames by the Thai people. Prior to the war, family names were not used in Siam, but the king decreed that all his subjects should adopt one. Women were also encouraged to grow their hair long, and the game of football was even introduced, with a royal team.

The genteel world of Siam was rocked once more in 1932, when a group of army officers staged a bloodless revolution, which brought the monarchy's absolute supremacy to an end. The authorities of Siam (by then renamed Thailand) signed friendship agreements with the Japanese in 1940. The following year, the Japanese invaded Thailand, and the Thais – seeing further resistance as hopeless – entered World War II soon afterwards on the side of the Axis. It was at this time that the notorious Death Railway was built, with its bridge over the River Kwai. Despite the fact that Thailand ended the war on the losing side, it was later allowed to join the United Nations due to a legal loophole in the original declaration of war.

Since 1932, continual political turbulence has beset Thailand. It has endured 19 coups, and while over 33 prime ministers have been appointed, only one of them has lasted a full term. Ironically though, Thailand is deemed one of the most stable countries in the region. It sided with the US during the Vietnam War, and throughout its history it has remained resolutely monarchist and equally resolutely anti-communist.

Largely thanks to tourism, Thailand saw rapid economic growth during the 1980s and 1990s. Unfortunately, in 1997,

Coup de Grâce

Of all the attempted military coups in Thailand (and there have been 19 in total), that which took place in 1950 must be recorded as one of the most bizarre. In May of that year, Prime Minister Phibul Songkhram was forced at gunpoint onto a naval ship moored in the Chao Phraya River. Negotiations failed to break the deadlock, and loyal forces launched an air and ground attack on the vessel. Fearing for the safety of their respected hostage, Phibul's captors helped him to swim to shore. Once there he telephoned headquarters, was picked up, and returned to power intact.

an unstable market crashed, and this resulted in the devaluation of the *baht* and in many local businesses going bankrupt. Tourism was dealt another blow by the December 2004 tsunami, which claimed 8,000 lives along Thailand's Andaman coast. Thankfully much of the damage was repaired within a year and the industry is now back in full swing.

In 1992 more than 100 pro-democracy demonstrators were wounded and killed by the military in the wake of massive protests that called for the resignation of non-elected Prime Minister Suchinda Kraprayoon. These events jolted the country to the brink of chaos and were only resolved by the intervention of King Bhumipol, the reigning monarch, who advocated reconciliation among the different parties. Following the king's intervention, a series of stable, democratically elected governments endured for the next 14 years.

In 2000 the newly formed Thai Rak Thai party, led by Thaksin Shinawatra, won a landslide victory. Despite being re-elected in 2005, Thaksin was dogged by allegations of corruption. Opposition parties boycotted the snap elections held in April 2006, and although Thaksin won again, he resigned in the face of mass protests.

Guard on duty at the Grand Palace

Thaksin's administration returned as a caretaker government a month later. This led to massive demonstrations and a sudden military coup in September 2006, which ousted Thaksin. The junta promised to hold elections within a year, but a series of bombings in Bangkok on New Year's Eve suggested that some parties might be trying to force the military's hand.

Historical Landmarks

1st century AD The Dvavarati culture is founded by the Mon people.

7–11th century The Khmers invade the country from the east.

1238 Thais establish an independent nation based at Sukhothai.

circa 1290 Rise of the Lanna kingdom in the north under King Mengrai.

1351 The kingdom of Ayutthaya is founded in the south.

1431 Ayutthaya conquers the Khmer empire centred on Angkor.

1767 Ayutthaya is invaded by the old enemy, Burma. General Taksin escapes and is crowned king the following year in Thonburi.

1782 In the new capital Bangkok, General Chao Phaya Chakri proclaims himself Rama I, the first king of the Chakri dynasty.

1851–68 King Mongkut (Rama IV) ascends the throne.

1868–1910 Chulalongkorn (Rama V) continues his father's initiatives.

1910–25 Rama VI (Vajiravudh) concentrates on political reforms. Britain persuades Siam to fight with the Allies in World War I.

1932 After a military coup Siam becomes a constitutional monarchy.

1939 Under Prime Minister Phibul Songkhram, Siam adopts a more militaristic stance. The country's name is changed to Thailand.

1939–45 During World War II, Thailand initially supports Japan in the conquest of Burma and Malaya, but later sides with the Allies.

1946 King Ananda dies in mysterious circumstances. His younger brother Bhumibol accedes to the throne as Rama IX.

1945–73 During the Vietnam War, the USA uses Thailand as a base.

1973–92 Internal politics are dominated by power struggles between the generals and civilian politicians.

1992 Demonstrations following the election of General Suchinda are violently suppressed The king intervenes, forcing Suchinda to resign.

1997–2001 Catastrophic economic collapse followed by gradual recovery. Democrat government led by Chuan Leekpai.

2004 The Asian tsunami strikes southern Thailand on 26 December.

2006 Opposition parties boycott April elections. A coup unseats Thaksin and installs a temporary military government.

2007 Nine bombs rock Bangkok in apparent opposition to military rule.

WHERE TO GO

BANGKOK

Thailand's capital might well come as a shock to the senses, but there is plenty to see for anyone prepared to put up with the heat and confusion. From its huge shopping malls, shady temples and bustling markets to its restaurants, sleepy canals and brazen nightlife, Bangkok offers endless surprises. King Rama I modelled the city after Ayutthaya, with its canals that crisscross the capital and its magnificent temples. Much of the old town has been replaced by the bursting metropolis, but there are still beautiful temples as well as palaces, historic buildings and, of course, Bangkok's notorious nightclubs.

The great distances and the heat make it one of the world's least walkable cities, and aimless sauntering may result in nothing but a twisted ankle, for the pavement is chronically torn up. Three preferable options are to find yourself a taxi, a *tuk-tuk* (a three-wheeled passenger carrying motor scooter) or a coach tour, which can be arranged in any hotel. There are also two new mass transit systems – called the Metro or subway (an underground network) and Skytrain (an elevated service) – which enable you to circumnavigate the city in air-conditioned comfort. Both operate frequently between key points such as Hualamphong, Silom Road, Sukhumvit Road and the hotels by the river *(see pages 122–3)*.

City Districts

Before you set out to explore the city, buy a map. Only with an extremely detailed and up-to-date city plan will you be able to take on the unplanned chaos that is Bangkok. What's

Detail of the Dusit Maha Prasat at the Grand Palace *(see page 26)*

more, don't expect to find a town centre, for the city's sights are widely spread, with several major neighbourhoods vying for attention. Start your tour with the area called **Ko Rattanakosin**, which has the greatest monuments and is situated just a stone's throw from the Chao Phraya River. This is the oldest part of the city, and is home to the magnificent Wat Phra Kaew and Grand Palace complex *(see page 26)*, as well as Wat Pho.

To the south is located one of Bangkok's original shopping centres. The **New Road** (also known as Charoen Krung Road) runs around the General Post Office and was the first official road in Thailand. This area is still well supplied with gift shops and 'instant' tailors. Several churches and embassies are situated between Charoen Krung and the river, as is the celebrated Oriental Hotel, once the haunt of such luminaries as Joseph Conrad, Noel Coward and Somerset Maugham.

Long tail boats on the Chao Phraya River

You may not find celebrities in **Chinatown** (the lively district off Charoen Krung), but you will see a profusion of entrepreneurs. Take a walk along Sampeng Lane (Soi Wanit 1), with its shops that sell Chinese lanterns, wigs, shark's-fin soup and gold necklaces. Follow this with a visit to the busy markets on the Rachawong and Yaowarat roads.

Khao San Road

Cinemas, cafés, restaurants and boutiques populate **Siam Square**, a low-rise grid of shopping arcades and streets fashionable with the young, with four- and five-storey air-conditioned shopping centres alongside. Look out for the city's most important spirit house on the corner of Ratchadamri Road and Ploenchit Road. The **Erawan Shrine** was built by the owners of the former Erawan Hotel following various mishaps, the final straw being the sinking at sea of a ship bringing marble to the hotel. There have been no further incidents since the shrine was finished, and today a steady stream of the faithful arrive to offer flowers and carved wooden elephants to the resident spirit.

Further east, across the railway tracks, Ploenchit Road becomes **Sukhumvit Road**. This marks the start of a rambling shopping, entertainment and residential area. Be warned: if you are trying to find somewhere specific, all the side roads *(soi)* have numbers as opposed to names, and wherever you go it is imperative that you have the full numerical address.

To the south, along Silom Road, is the business district and **Patpong**, a small plot of land that started as a rice terrace and is now the most famous of the city's red-light strips.

Visiting tips

If visiting the Wat Phra Kaew and Grand Palace, make sure you allow at least a couple of hours and don't forget that respectful dress (no sleeveless T-shirts, shorts skirts or shorts) is required and the guards at the main entrance vigorously enforce this dress code. For a small fee you can borrow a long skirt.

Wat Phra Kaew and Grand Palace Complex

If you have time for only one sight in Bangkok, make it the **Wat Phra Kaew and Grand Palace** complex (open daily 8.30am–3.30pm; admission fee also covers Vimanmek, *see page 32*; tel: 0 2623 5500), to the east of the river, near **Tha Chang** pier. No other temple so typifies Thai art as the Wat Phra Kaew, the Temple of the Emerald Buddha. Its glittering surfaces and wealth of art make it one of Asia's architectural wonders.

Wat Phra Kaew was the first major complex to be built in Bangkok. As you enter the compound, you will encounter an imposing trio of structures to your left – the huge golden **Phra Si Rattana Chedi**, the **Phra Mondop** (Library of Buddhist Scriptures), and the **Prasat Phra Thep Bidom** (Royal Pantheon). Behind the Phra Mondop is a large sandstone model of Angkor Wat. Along the northern edge of the model, you will also find **Viharn Yot** (Prayer Hall), flanked by **Ho Phra Nak** (Royal Mausoleum) on the left and **Ho Phra Montien Tham** (Auxillary Library) on the right.

Next you will come to the **Chapel of the Emerald Buddha**, which was specially constructed to house the kingdom's most sacred image, the Emerald Buddha. Sitting high on a pedestal, the 66-cm (26-in) tall jadeite image is surprisingly small, but the fact that it is venerated in such a lavish manner leaves no doubt as to its importance to the Thais.

From Wat Phra Kaew, turn left into the adjacent **Grand Palace**, where the first building of note is the **Amarin Vinitchai Throne Hall**, which served as a royal residence for the first three kings of the Chakri dynasty: Rama I, II and III. Built during the reign of Rama I, the hall contains two thrones, the upper in the shape of a boat, the lower covered by a magnificent nine-tiered white canopy.

Next is the majestic **Chakri Maha Prasat** (Grand Palace Hall). It was built in 1882 by the internationally minded Rama V, and blends Asian and Italian Renaissance styles. The approach stairway and central balcony are of particular note. These are topped by a traditional roof, which rises in stages to three seven-tiered spires. Below the central spire stands a golden urn containing the ashes of the Chakri kings.

Further on the left, a pair of 200-year-old stone lions stand guard at the entrance to the **Dusit Maha Prasat** (Dusit Hall), where kings used to conduct state business. It is now the final resting place for deceased kings before they are cremated in the nearby Sanam Luang field.

The Chakri Maha Prasat, centrepiece of the Grand Palace

On the edge of the square, near the Dusit Hall, you will see an elegant white marble building known as the **Arporn Phimok Prasat** (Disrobing Pavilion). Built to the height of the king's palanquin, this was where the king would alight from his carriage and adjust his ceremonial hat before finally proceeding into the throne hall.

Just opposite is the **Wat Phra Kaew Museum**, which has a collection of exquisite Buddha images made of crystal, silver, ivory and gold as well as some beautiful lacquer screens.

On the way out you can also visit the **Coins and Decorations Museum**. Displayed in glass cases in two jail-like enclaves are gold coins, swords and crown jewels, all dating from the 11th century.

Six Great Wats

Visit six of Bangkok's *wats* – monasteries or temples – as part of your tour of its greatest architectural wonders, but do make sure that you leave plenty of time, as distances between them can be quite considerable.

What's a Wat?

You will see *wats*, or Buddhist temples, everywhere in Thailand. To help you find your way around, here's a brief rundown of the most common architectural terms:

bot: the main sanctuary of a temple, where religious rites are held

viharn: a replica of the bot that is used to keep Buddha images

prang: an ellipse-shaped stupa based on the corner tower of a Khmer temple and also housing images of the Buddha

chedi (stupa): the most venerated structure, a bell-like dome that originally enshrined relics of the Buddha, later of holy men and kings

mondop: wood or brick structure with pyramidal roof, built as a repository for a holy object

One of the best-known Thai landmarks, **Wat Arun** (Temple of Dawn; across from Tha Tien Pier; open daily 8.30am–5.30pm; admission fee; tel: 0 2891 1149), stands on the opposite bank of the Chao Phraya River in Thonburi, but is only a minute or two away by ferry. The temple was built during the first half of the 19th century by Rama II and Rama III, and is decorated with millions of fragments of porcelain arranged in the shape of flowers. The

Wat Pho, Bangkok's
oldest temple

central tower affords stunning views across the river. For quintessential sunset views, photographers should best perch themselves at the riverside bar on the opposite bank.

Wat Pho (open daily 8am–6pm; admission fee; tel: 0 2221 5910), Bangkok's oldest temple, houses an incredible 19th-century gilt reclining Buddha in its vast white enclosure. Almost 15m (49ft) high and 46m (151ft) long, it reaches right up to the roof of the temple. On the feet, inlaid with mother-of-pearl, are the 108 auspicious characteristics of the Buddha.

A tall teak structure painted red and called the Giant Swing stands incongruously outside the monastery of **Wat Suthat** (Bamrung Muang Road; open daily 8.30am–5.30pm; admission fee; tel: 0 2224 9845). In former years, death-defying swingers used to show off their acrobatic skills during the annual Brahmin harvest festival. The show has not been held since 1935, however, when it was stopped after several of the faithful lost their balance. Don't miss one of the city's

The Buddha at Wat Traimit, Thailand's largest gold image

most beautiful (and largest) Buddhas at the temple nearby. Outside, graceful bronze horses stand at the four corners of the building.

The **Golden Mount**, accessed via **Wat Saket** (Boriphat Road; open daily 8am–5pm; admission fee), can be seen long before you reach it. It sits atop Bangkok's only hill – and an artificial one at that – surmounted by a big gold *chedi* (stupa). Spiral steps up the mount's reinforced sides lead to a viewing platform. Take a map with you to identify the palaces and temples spread out below the summit. The faithful make the climb less for the view than for the shrine containing relics of the Buddha. These were given to King Rama V in 1897 by Lord Curzon, Viceroy of India.

The best time to visit **Wat Benjamabophit**, the Marble Temple (Rama V Road; open daily 8am–5.30pm; admission fee; tel: 0 2282 7413), is at dawn, when the graceful marble is still tinged with orange and the monks are lining up for their daily alms. Built at the turn of the 20th century, it is one of the finest examples of recent temple architecture in the city. It is a haven of calm, with its inner courtyard surrounded by Buddha statues, and its ponds filled with plump fish and turtles, fed daily with papaya and bananas by the monks. Outside and past the canal are the monks' quarters, set among lawns.

The impressive Buddha at **Wat Traimit** (Traimit Road; open daily 8am–5pm; admission fee; tel: 0 2225 9775) might have remained concealed forever had it not been for workmen extending the port of Bangkok, who dropped the then stucco-covered statue from a crane, revealing the vast Buddha inside. This is Thailand's largest gold image, weighing 4.5 metric tonnes (5 tons) and dating from the Sukhothai period, when it was probably disguised to keep it out of the hands of the warring Burmese.

Museums and Palaces

On Na Phra That Road, a short walk from the Grand Palace, stands the **National Museum** (open Wed–Sun 9am–4pm; admission fee; tel: 0 2224 1333; <www.thailandmuseum.com>). The museum houses Thailand's finest collection of antiquities. The sculpture, ceramics and jewellery exhibited here offer an insight into the country's unique synthesis of different cultures – as well as the sheer variety of the kingdom's artefacts. Try to be there for a tour (ask at Tourism Authority offices for times) so as not to be overwhelmed by the museum's size and scope.

The exhibition divides Thai culture into several periods, starting off with the Dvaravati (6th–11th century AD), then tracing the development of political power to Lan Na, Sukhothai, Ayutthaya and ultimately Bangkok. The rooms are arranged in a chronological fashion, and you can see the changes in the portrayal of the Buddha, the overriding theme of Thai art, as you walk through.

The museum offers a range of other things to see, from an 18-metric tonne (20-ton) royal funeral chariot – which needed over 290 people to push it – to thrones, litters, 19th-century Thai typewriters, and even a

Museum highlight

The earliest works in the National Museum – from excavations at Ban Chiang in Northeast Thailand – are the most interesting: pots and jars with bold designs in the shape of fingerprints. The haunting patterns are curiously modern, and yet the pottery is probably 5,000 years old.

Carving from Ayutthaya at
Jim Thompson's House

full-sized model elephant fitted out for battle.

A different sort of museum is situated in the magnificent **Jim Thompson's House**, located to the east of the city (Soi Kasemsan 2, off Rama I Road; open daily 9am–5pm; admission fee includes a compulsory guided tour; tel: 0 2216 7368; <www.jimthompsonhouse.com>). Bringing a sense of calm even to the most frenetic of days, the cool timber rooms of this teak house are packed with priceless artefacts, sculptures and ceramics.

The story of Jim Thompson is as intriguing as his taste in art. A New York architect, he came to Southeast Asia as a secret agent in World War II. Settling in Bangkok after the war, he converted the Thai silk industry from a primitive craft into an international big business. In 1967 he vanished while on holiday in neighbouring Malaysia. The mystery of his disappearance is still unsolved. No trace of Thompson has ever been found, but this monument, 'the house on the *khlong*' (canal), is exactly as he left it.

The huge palace **Vimanmek** ('Celestial Residence'; open daily 9.30am–4pm; admission fee or free with Grand Palace entrance ticket; tel: 0 2628 6300), in Dusit Park off Ratchawithi Road, might lack mystery, but it's certainly not short of scale. Built during King Chulalongkorn's reign, it is reputedly the largest teak building in the world, and contains an impressive collection of objets d'art, paintings and royal jewellery, plus the first shower ever installed in Thailand. The palace has been restored under the patronage of Queen Sirikit.

One final building not to be missed is the **Suan Pakkad Palace** on Sri Ayutthaya Road (open daily 9am–4pm; admission fee; tel: 0 2245 4934), near the Phaya Thai skytrain station. This superb building is owned by Princess Chumbot and surrounded by leafy gardens. Down at the bottom of the impeccable garden stands the delightful **Lacquer Pavilion**, which is believed to be the only house of its type to survive the sack of Ayutthaya in 1767. Bought in 1959, the pavilion was then rebuilt here as a gift to the princess from her late husband. Some of the inside walls are covered with exquisite paintings – in gold leaf on black lacquer – which illustrate scenes in the life of the Buddha and episodes from the national legend, the *Ramakien*. Suan Pakkad literally translates as 'lettuce garden'.

Vimanmek Palace, a splendid teak-built residence

Bangkok Afloat

The most popular way of exploring the fascinating *khlong* (canals), which are so central to Bangkok's character, is to take either a tour from Tha Chang pier near the Grand Palace, or a similar trip arranged by any of the hotels. A one-hour tour is quite expensive, but will take you to sections of old Thonburi that you would hardly dream still existed – past floating restaurants and petrol stations, old wooden houses and temples.

Most river tours leave early in the morning and include a visit to the **Royal Barges National Museum** (open daily 9am–5pm; admission fee; tel: 0 2424 0004) in their shed in Khlong Bangkok Noi. The otherworldly ceremonial craft are trimmed with fanciful prows and elaborate red and gold decorations. The king's own boat is propelled by 50 oarsmen.

You can explore the canals on your own by means of the local boats, called *hang yao*. These long, narrow craft,

Exploring a *khlong* by boat

powered by noisy truck engines, carry the propeller on the end of a long drive shaft – hence their name, which means 'long-tailed' boats. You can also hire your own *hang yao* by the hour, but be sure to agree on a price in advance.

Down Khlong Bangkok Noi (Small Canal) and Khlong Yai (Big Canal), handsome houses with gardens and fountains are squeezed cheek by jowl with old, wooden houses on stilts, shaded by palm trees. Nearby you will see rubber tyre factories next to temples, floating markets and snack bars.

If you prefer slower and cheaper transport, take the **Chao Phraya Tourist Boat** (operates daily 9.30am–3pm; tel: 0 2623 6143; <www.chaophrayaboat.co.th>), which costs 100 *baht*. The route begins at Tha Sathorn and travels upriver to Tha Phra Athit, with stops at 10 major piers along the way. Boats leave every 30 minutes, and you can get off at any pier and pick up another boat later. After 3pm, you can use the ticket on the Chao Phraya River Express Boat, which runs at 15-minute intervals between 6am and 6.40pm. The express boats travel between Tha Nonthaburi pier in the north and ends at Tha Wat Rachasingkhon near Krungthep Bridge in the south.

Other Sights

Don't forget to bring your camera to **Chatuchak Weekend Market**, for this is the most extensive and mind-boggling collection of stalls that you can imagine. Anything from wigs to potted plants and herbal cures for insomnia is available. Take note, though: Chatuchak is open only on Saturdays and Sundays, from dawn to dusk.

The **Queen Saovabha Memorial Institute** (open 8.30am–4pm on weekdays, 8.30am–noon on holidays; admission fee; tel: 0 2252 0164), more popularly known as **Snake Farm**, is operated by the Red Cross. Its primary function is to produce anti-venom serum, from seven types of snakes, to be used on snakebite victims. Tourists may view the venom milking sessions, which take place from Mondays to Fridays at 11am and 2.30pm, and on Saturdays and Sundays at 11am.

The Thais themselves don't come to **Dusit Zoo** (open daily 8.30am–6pm; admission fee; tel: 0 2281 2000) to see the wildlife in its natural habitat, but to watch the less than natural sight of elephants and deer begging for food. In the off-colour pond, where romantic couples go boating, giant turtles even try to consume Coca-Cola bottles. Apart from the animals and admirably landscaped aviary, the zoo is probably the best place in Bangkok to watch the Thai people having fun.

Lumphini Park (open daily 4.30am–8pm; free) is a relative haven of peace in the city centre. Thais come here at the weekend to picnic and indulge in the art of *sanuk* (having a good time). In addition to stalls selling kebabs and noodles, there is a bar and restaurant at the park's northern exit (leading to Soi Sarasin) from where you can watch the sun go down.

Feeding the birds in Lumphini Park

EXCURSIONS FROM BANGKOK

The following excursions are all easily reached from Bangkok, and make rewarding side trips or useful stepping stones on the way north or south.

Rose Garden and Nakhon Pathom

One hour's drive to the west of Bangkok's heat and tumult lies the cool and calm **Rose Garden Riverside Resort** (open daily 8am–6pm; admission fee; tel: 0 3432 2588; <www.rose-garden.com>). The roses form only a small part of the 28-hectare (70-acre) tropical garden. A cultural performance is staged daily at 2.45pm and features folk and classical dances, sword fights, Thai boxing and a traditional Thai wedding.

From the Rose Garden, continue 30km (20 miles) west to **Nakhon Pathom** (widely believed to be Thailand's oldest town), home to **Phra Pathom Chedi**, the largest *chedi* (stupa) in the country. King Mongkut built this pagoda, which resembles an upside-down ice cream cone, in the middle of the 19th century on top of the ruins of an ancient temple dating back over 1,000 years. During the 1970s, this new *chedi* almost collapsed, but the Fine Arts Department took prompt action and fortunately saved the day, so that it can still be seen in all its glory.

Floating Market

You won't need a guide to show you the way to the floating market at **Damnoen Saduak** (daily 7am–1pm), as everyone runs tours there nowadays. Even so, the diminutive boats, which are

Sanam Chan Palace

Also at Nakhon Pathom is the Sanam Chan Palace. This early 20th-century structure is in traditional Thai style, with the exception of one English Tudor building, which was once used as a setting for performances of Shakespeare plays.

Boats piled high with produce at the Floating Market

piled high with coconuts, bananas and durian, remain – almost – as authentic as ever. Try to get there quite early, while the women in broad-brimmed hats are still out in full force, paddling along the narrow canals and haggling for a bunch of chillies or some barbecued fish. Photographers might want to walk along the edge of the canal, or stop on the wooden bridges, which make excellent spots for observation. For a few hundred *baht*, a boat can even be arranged to paddle you out into the centre of the fray. At another tourist market onshore you can buy Burmese carpets, wood carvings and other such things. However, the goods are expensive, on the whole, and you will often find that identical goods are sold at keener prices in shops in Bangkok or in Chiang Mai's Night Market.

Kanchanaburi

Kanchanaburi's calm, lush setting on the banks of the **Kwai River** belies its history, for it was here during World War II that thousands of prisoners of war died building the famous **bridge on the River Kwai**, as recounted in Pierre Boulle's novel and the film based on it. The current structure was rebuilt after the war, and only the eight curved sections on it are original. Two trains cross the bridge every day on their way to the town of **Nam Tok** (Waterfall), a pleasant hour's journey further to the west. You can walk across the bridge or view it from the long-tailed boats that hurtle up and down the river, stopping off at the cemetery and nearby caves.

To get an idea of the horrors of building the bridge, visit the two cemeteries, which contain over 8,000 graves of British, Dutch, Australian, Malaysian, Indian, Canadian, New Zealander and Burmese prisoners and conscripts who died during the railway's construction, along with around 100,000 Asian civilians. The inscriptions on the gravestones are as simple and moving as tragic poems.

Afterwards, you can drop in at the **JEATH War Museum** (open daily 8.30am–6pm; admission fee) on the riverbank. Housed in a type of bamboo hut used in the prison camps, the exhibition documents Japanese atrocities in photographs, paintings and relics. It also reveals the prisoners' ingenuity in surviving great hardships, and also the sympathy and help

Visitors pay their respects at the bridge on the River Kwai

Scenery at Sangkhlaburi

secretly offered to the inmates by local people.

At the **Thailand-Burma Railway Centre** (open daily 9am–5pm, admission fee, tel: 0 3451 0067), located south of the bridge, there are exhibits on the history of the Death Railway and even a full-scale replica of the original bridge.

Sangkhlaburi

There are bases for tourists northwest of Kanchanaburi, making it easier for the exploration of some of the most unspoilt scenery in the country. One hotel next to the river pampers its guests with air-conditioning and a swimming pool, while a couple of others, slightly more spartan, are built on bamboo rafts floating in the stream. Excursions to waterfalls, caves and national parks, including **Erawan National Park** (open daily 8.30am–4.30pm; admission fee; tel: 0 3457 4222; <www.dnp.go.th>), can be arranged from these camps.

Some distance upstream from the Sai Yok National Park lies **Hellfire Pass**, christened by POWs who were forced to dig in this area by torchlight. The road to **Sangkhlaburi** runs between the densely forested mountain slopes of the national parks, passing Khao Laem Reservoir, with the town situated at the northern tip of the lake. Sangkhlaburi is an ideal base for elephant trekking expeditions to nearby Mon and Karen villages. The **Three Pagodas Pass**, 12km (7½ miles) further on, lies at an altitude of 1,400m (4,480ft). It owes its name to the three little white *chedis* erected here in the 18th century.

Ayutthaya

The most enjoyable way of visiting the ancient capital of Ayutthaya, 88km (55 miles) north of Bangkok, is by incorporating a trip on the Chao Phraya River. The River Sun Cruise (tel: 0 2266 9125, <www.riversuncruise.co.th>) organises daily trips to Ayutthaya, leaving at 8am by air-conditioned coach from the River City Shopping Complex and returning to the pier in front of it, by a converted rice barge. On the way you will see rice fields and the beginnings of the countryside that stretches to Nakhon Sawan, and factories and warehouses.

Before exploring the great archaeological site itself, most tours stop at the nearby royal estate of **Bang Pa-In** (open daily 8am–4.30pm; admission fee; tel: 0 3526 1673). This collection of palaces, set in gardens, was built by King Chulalongkorn in the late 19th century. The names of palaces like 'the Excellent and Shining Abode' and 'the Sage's Lookout' are as delightful as the structures themselves. Nothing beats the splendid **Aisawan Thipha-at** (The Divine Seat of Personal Freedom) in the middle of the lake by which King Chulalongkorn (Rama V) composed odes as the sun went down.

Back on the highway, continue 20km (12½ miles) north to the town of **Ayutthaya**, former capital of Thailand

Wat Phra Sri Sanphet

and home to one of its greatest civilisations. Here, where cattle still graze, you can climb up the steps of ruined temples to look over the immensity of the ruined city, which was laid waste by the Burmese, who sacked the capital in 1767.

There are dozens of distinctive buildings, and you will be hard-pressed to visit Ayutthaya in one day. For a tour of the ruins, it's best to start at **Wat Phra Sri Sanpet** (open daily 8am–5pm; admission fee), on Si Sanphet Road, near the tourist parking area. The temple was built in 1491 and once housed a 16-m (52-ft) Buddha image covered in gold and weighing 250kg (551 lbs). In 1767 the Burmese set fire to the statue in order to melt off the gold, destroying both temple and image. What you can see are restored *chedis* (stupas) which hold the ashes of King Borom Trai Lokanat and his two sons.

At **Wat Phra Ram** (open daily 8am–5pm, admission fee), a graceful 14th-century building positioned amid reflecting pools, there is a beautiful cloister lined with stone Buddha images, as well as several elephant gates, mythical creatures called *naga* and *garuda*. The temple was built in 1369 by King Ramesuan, on the site where his father was cremated.

Founding a Dynasty

According to Thai legend, Ayutthaya was founded by the illegitimate son of a princess, who was discovered to be pregnant after eating an aubergine on which a gardener had relieved himself! U-Thong, or Prince of the Golden Crib as the son was named, became the first of 33 ruling kings, while the kingdom became the largest and most beautiful in the East as well as the principal kingdom in Siam for over four centuries.

Next, visit **Wat Phra Ma-hathat** (open daily 8am–6pm; admission fee), one of the most beautiful temple complexes in Ayutthaya; it dates from the 1380s. Once it held treasures of precious stones, gold and crystal, and a relic of the Lord Buddha in a gold casket, which is now housed in the National Museum in Bangkok *(see page 31)*. **Wat Ratchaburana** (open daily 8am–5pm; admission fee), next to Wat Ma-hathat, was built in the 15th

A surviving stone Buddha

century around the tombs of Prince Ai and Prince Yo, brothers who slew each other in a tragic battle on elephant back. Rare frescoes remain in the crypt, but any portable antiquities were stolen or removed to museums years ago.

For an overview of Ayutthayan-style art, visit the **Chao Sam Phraya National Museum** (open Wed–Sun 9am–4pm; admission fee; tel: 0 3524 1587), which is stocked with well preserved statues recovered from the ruins. There are beautiful bronze Buddhas dating from the 13th and 14th centuries; 17th- and 18th-century door panels with religious, traditional or floral carvings, and a hoard of 15th-century gold jewellery.

Finish off with a visit to the **elephant *kraal***, a few miles from town, where hunters used to drive large herds of up to 200 wild elephants into the stockade. Once captured, they were put into the king's service as fighters or, if they were the rare white type, as symbols of power. The last capture was in 1903 during the reign of King Chulalongkorn.

Ancient City

If your time is limited, there is no need to go to Sukhothai and Ayutthaya in order to see the ancient capitals. A temple buff has made the trip unnecessary by building models of them in what is said to be the world's largest outdoor museum, 33km (20 miles) southeast of Bangkok. Laid out like a map of Thailand, covering roughly 80 hectares (200 acres), **Ancient City** or Muang Boran (open daily 8am–5pm; admission fee; tel: 0 2323 9253) re-creates the country's greatest buildings in full size or at a slightly reduced scale. The parks also feature exotic birds, monkeys and elephants. Travel agents run half-day outings here, and there are daily buses from Bangkok.

Crocodile Farm and Zoo

Another 5km (3 miles) along the road from Ancient City is the **Samut Prakan Crocodile Farm & Zoo** (open daily 7am–

Samut Prakan Crocodile Farm and Zoo

6pm; admission fee; tel: 0 2703 4891; <www.paknam.com>). This huge enclosure is billed as the world's largest establishment of its kind, with the total 'croc' population put at almost 60,000. The farm preserves endangered species at the same time it entertains and educates the public. There is also a zoo featuring exotic birds, tigers, chimpanzees, ostriches, camels and elephants, as well as a Dinosaur Musueum.

Khao Yai National Park

Khao Yai (open daily 8am–6pm; admission fee; tel: 0 3731 9002; <www.dnp.go.th>) rises from the Khorat plateau northeast of Bangkok, baked dry in summer and verdant after the rains. Khao Yai means 'big mountain', and the resort, located three hours' drive from Bangkok (200km/125 miles), is the oldest and one of the best in the land. The park can be reached by taking the bus from Bangkok to Pak Chong in Nakhon Ratchasima province, where there are pick-ups that leave for the main entrance.

The national park covers 2,100 sq km (837 sq miles). Within its boundaries are elephants and over 100 other species, including Asian wild dog, clouded leopard and black bear. Keep an eye out for some of Thailand's most significant bird concentrations, among which are some of the largest groups of hornbills in Southeast Asia, moustached barbets, orange-breasted and red-headed trogons and great slaty woodpeckers. Wildlife sightings are not consistently common or guaranteed, but the walks to giant waterfalls are pleasant. Night-time safaris employ spotlights to locate deer, tropical birds and – if you're lucky – tigers and bears.

Before being declared a national park in 1962, Khao Yai was known as a sanctuary not just for animals, but also as a popular hiding place for outlaws. This, of course, is no longer the case, and now the park offers hotels, a restaurant and an 18-hole golf course.

THAILAND'S 'KHMER CULTURE TRAIL'

About 250km (100 miles) from Bangkok is the provincial capital of Khorat, **Nakhon Ratchasima**. The richest and largest city in the northeast, it is a good jumping off point for excursions to the Khmer ruins of the Khorat Plateau, including Phimai, Phanom Rung and Prasat Muang Tam.

Phimai

Phimai, 60km (37 miles) north of Nakhon Ratchasima, is known for its ancient religious compound at the end of the long, dusty main street. Probably built during King Suriyavarman I's reign in the 11th century, and situated not too far from the Cambodian border, Phimai was designed by Khmer architects, and predates the magnificent Angkor Wat in Cambodia. Four gates dominate the ruins, the largest preceded by a bridge guarded by lions. Adorning the elegant arcades of the cloisters are intricate engravings of flowers, elephants and monkeys.

In the inner courtyard stand two small *prangs* (Prang Hin Daeng and Prang Phromathat), and in the centre there is an ornate dome with doors and a lintel, intricately carved with scenes related to Mahayana Buddhism. Outside in the gardens there is an open-air museum, with a collection of ancient friezes, statues and stone lintels showing Buddha, gods and monkeys.

Banyan tree

A pleasant way to round off the trip to Phimai is to visit the banyan tree, which stands 2km (1 mile) further down the road and is said to be the biggest in Thailand. Delicious Isaan food is served in its shade, but only in the dry season – during the wet season, the nearby reservoir floods the picnic ground. If spirits live in trees – as many Thais believe – then this prodigious banyan is surely thronged with ghosts.

Phanom Rung

Phimai may be the best-known and most easily accessible Khmer temple site in Northeast Thailand, but Buriram's **Prasat Hin Khao Phanom Rung** is better preserved, and set in more spectacular scenery atop an extinct volcano. Phanom Rung was constructed between the 10th and 13th centuries, but the greater part of the work was completed in the reign of King Suriyavarman II (1112–52), during the period when the architecture of Angkor reached its apogee. Today, after painstaking restoration, the sanctuary is the largest and best-preserved of all Thailand's Khmer monuments.

Phanom Rung was originally built as a Hindu temple honouring the deities Vishnu and Shiva. Beautifully carved representations of these two gods can be found in the lintels and pediments of the sanctuary, together with figures of Nandi, the bull mount of Shiva and Uma. On the east portico of the antechamber to the main sanctuary is a fine Nataraja, or Dancing Shiva figure.

The spectacular Phanom Rung

Prasat Muang Tam

About 8km (5 miles) south of Phanom Rung, in the dusty plain approaching the Cambodian frontier, stands the old Khmer sanctuary of **Prasat Muang Tam**. Fifteen years ago Muang Tam was a lopsided mass of stone walls and

Prasat Kamphaeng Yai

lintels, shrouded in the dense vegetation of centuries of neglect. Today the temple complex has been splendidly restored by the Archaeological Commission of Thailand.

Other Gems

Additional gems in the 'Khmer Culture Trail' can be found in the neighbouring provinces of Surin and Si Saket. **Ban Pluang**, which dates from the second half of the 11th century and was once an important stop on the road between Angkor and Phimai, is a square sandstone tower built on a laterite platform. The surrounding moats and ponds have been turned into an attractive garden. Nearby **Sikhoraphum**, also carefully restored, consists of five brick *prangs* on a square laterite platform surrounded by lily-filled ponds. The lintel and pillars of the central *prang (see box on page 28)* are beautifully carved with heavenly dancing girls, or *apsaras*, and other scenes from Hindu mythology.

Prasat Kamphaeng Yai

The 'Khmer Culture Trail' ends with the heavy laterite sanctuary of **Prasat Kamphaeng Yai**. Here the ancient Khmer ruins rub shoulders with a much more recent Thai temple, and saffron-robed monks may be seen eating, studying or contemplating in the shade of the massive, attenuated *prangs*. Although the Khmer sanctuary was originally dedicated to the Hindu god Vishnu, the overall effect is most pleasing, and the active Buddhist presence strangely at one.

CENTRAL THAILAND

The most striking feature of the central region is its sheer abundance. This vast, fertile plain that starts at Bangkok's busy outskirts is the country's rice bowl, home to one-third of the population, and source of one of the world's biggest rice crops. Centuries ago, this agricultural heartland was also home to some of the kingdom's greatest civilisations, among them those of Si Satchanalai, Sukhothai and Lopburi, ancient cities that are as enchanting in ruins as they must have been in their heyday. In Central Thailand as well are two of the country's most popular beach resorts – Pattaya and Hua Hin, located 147km (91 miles) southeast and 203km (126 miles) southwest of Bangkok, respectively. Major towns are easily visited from Bangkok, and the ones to the north make good stopovers if you are en route to Thailand's northern region.

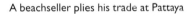

A beachseller plies his trade at Pattaya

Pattaya

Visitors no longer come to **Pattaya** for pristine beaches and tropical seas, for this infamous resort, located 147km (91 miles) southeast of Bangkok, lost its original attractions to pollution and development many years ago.

It was in the 1960s that the provincial seaside town rose to prominence. This was when the first American servicemen arrived from Vietnam War duties for what was soon described as 'R & R' – rest and recreation. The Thais eventually realised Pattaya's commercial possibilities, and the area fast became a thriving international resort.

Pattaya's transvestite shows are world famous

Today, Pattaya is noted for an abundance of accommodation, bars and clubs, and outdoor activities. Most hotels have swimming pools, since these days the sea around Pattaya Bay is not recommended. If swimming is what you are after, take a boat trip to the outlying coral islands. Or catch a bus to the beach at Jomtien, a 15-minute trip south, where clean sand stretches for miles, with gleaming condominiums as a backdrop.

The adventurous can try out parasailing, sailing, jet-skiing and water-skiing, while others may prefer a day's deep-sea fishing, relishing the opportunity to try catching delicious snapper and sizeable marlin. Excursion boats take tourists to islands in the surrounding area for swimming and snorkelling in clear blue seas.

At **Ko Larn** (about 45 minutes from Pattaya in a converted trawler or half the time in a speedboat) you can explore the underwater world in a glass-bottomed boat, gazing at vivid tropical fish and coral – albeit now sadly depleted. Many scuba expeditions begin here before going on to a couple of wrecks further south near Sattahip.

Land tours are just as easy to arrange. To the east, **Nong Nooch Tropical Garden** (open daily 8am–6pm; admission fee; tel: 0 3870 9358), 15km (9 miles) features daily displays of folk dances, martial arts and cockfighting, and a vast acreage of exotic palms, orchids and cacti. Alternatively, try **Pattaya Park** (open daily 9am–6pm; admission fee; tel: 0 3825 1201), a water theme park, or **Pattaya Elephant Village** (open daily 8.30am–7pm, admission fee, tel: 0 3824 9819), where elephants show off their strength, skill and obedience. For a strange cultural experience, visit Naklua's fantastic wood-carved **Sanctuary of Truth** (open daily 8am–6pm; admission fee; tel: 0 3836 7229), a 105-m (340-ft)-tall monument to Hindu-Buddhist philosophy built by one of Thailand's biggest car dealers. An adjacent lagoon offers dolphin shows and speedboat rides.

Pattaya offers abundant culinary delights. The restaurants serve first-rate seafood: there are plenty of simple waterfront restaurants that are rich in character but cheap in price. Those who prefer French fries and *bratwurst* shouldn't worry either.

Pattaya's nightlife, too, has something to satisfy almost all tastes, from big stage productions at Alangkarn Theatre and transvestite shows, to discotheques, nightclubs, beer bars – and all other establishments that have earned this area its reputation as the international entertainment resort of Thailand.

The Eastern Seaboard

Further east of Pattaya, the small idyllic island of **Ko Samet** has become a firm weekend favourite for Bangkok residents. The white sand beaches and clear blue water are part of a national marine park so most accommodation is fairly low key. The island is best avoided on public holidays, when visitors outnumber beds, and tents spring up everywhere.

Near the Cambodian border, Thailand's second-largest island, **Ko Chang** (Elephant Island), is the dominant isle of over 50 that make up the national marine park of the same name. A current development drive is gradually transforming the hilly island from a place of backpacker

Candlelight Beach on Ko Samet

bungalows to one consisting of higher-end boutique resorts, but it's still one of the most pristine islands in the Gulf of Thailand.

Hua Hin

You can easily bypass Pattaya and opt for quieter charms at **Hua Hin**, 220km (136 miles) southwest of Bangkok on the opposite shore of the Gulf of Thailand. A slew of condominiums and retirement homes are changing this former fishing village, and its long, sweeping beaches are no longer as pleasant as they once were for swimming. They do, however, make fine strolling ground, and with

its deckchairs to laze in,
pony-riding, golf courses
and luxurious spa retreats,
Hua Hin is far removed in
atmosphere from Pattaya.

Lopburi

Lopburi's dominant features
are the superb stone temples
built by the Khmers. These
can be spotted even from
the railway station, as can the
French-style architecture and
several hundred monkeys that

Lopburi's mischievous
primates will beg for food

have become this town's other lasting claim to fame.

Originally one of the capitals of the Khmer people, Lopburi flourished under Thai rule in the 17th century. King Narai chose the town as an alternative capital, in case some unforeseen fate befell Ayutthaya. His caution was justified: Ayutthaya was sacked by the Burmese the following century.

Begin your tour at **King Narai's Palace** or Phra Narai Ratchaniwet (open Wed–Sun 7am–5.30pm; admission fee), which was constructed in the mid-17th century, and took longer than 12 years to complete. Inside is the National Museum, housing exquisite examples of Khmer art. The palace also incorporates the old treasure houses, a banquet hall, an audience hall for high-ranking foreign visitors and stables.

After the palace, visit **Ban Vichayen** (open daily 6am–6pm; admission fee), which originally served as the residence of Chevalier de Chaumont, the first French ambassador to Thailand. Later it was the residence of Constantine Phaulkon (*see page 15*).

Near the railway station, **Wat Phra Si Rattana Mahathat** (open Wed–Sun 7am–5pm; admission fee) is a fine example of 12th-century Khmer-style architecture, with *chedis* built in Sukhothai style.

Lopburi's famous monkeys can be found by the railway in the Kala Shrine, as well as in nearby **Phra Prang Sam Yot** (open daily 8am–5pm; admission fee), a magnificent 13th-century temple with three distinctive *prangs* from which they like to hang, begging food and fruit from visitors. Make sure you keep firm hold of your camera and other valuables, as monkeys clutching stolen goods are a not uncommon sight.

Sukhothai

Sukhothai, the most striking of Thailand's various spectacular ruined cities, lies 427km (265 miles) north of Bangkok, surrounded by rice fields and distant hills. Built in the mid 13th and early 14th centuries under the legendary King Ramkamhaeng, Sukhothai flourished for

Lilies at Wat Sa Si, Sukhothai

almost 150 years until vanquished by Ayutthaya, and
its people fled. Until around
40 years ago, the ancient
capital was hidden by jungle, the outlines of the classical towers camouflaged by
heavy green undergrowth.
The situation is now better,
for in a huge renovation
programme implemented by
UNESCO and Thailand's gov-

Reaching Sukhothai

The Sukhothai ruins lie
within the boundaries of
the historical park, 13km
(8 miles) west of the new
town of Sukhothai, and are
reached easily by *songthaew*,
pick-up trucks with seats in
the back, which carry as
many passengers as can be
squeezed in.

ernment, some 200 moats, kilns, images and temples have
been partially restored to the glory of earlier days.

For a glimpse of some remarkable sculptures, start at the
Ramkamhaeng National Museum (open daily 9am–4pm;
admission fee; tel: 0 5561 2167), near the Kamphaeng Hek
Gate. This houses a splendid 14th-century example of the
Walking Buddha, which is, according to archaeologists, the
finest of all Thai Buddhas. A replica of King Ramkamhaeng's
famous inscription is also on show. This oft-repeated quo-
tation is the earliest example of Thai script and goes: 'In the
water there are fish, in the fields there is rice … those who
choose to laugh, laugh, those who choose to cry, cry.'

A short walk past the moat brings you to **Wat Mahathat**,
the Temple of the Great Relic. This is the biggest and finest temple in Sukhothai, dating from the 13th century and housing
rows of the standing Buddha images known as Phra Attharot.

Continue by visiting beautiful **Wat Sa Si** (Temple of the
Splendid Pond), with its graceful image of the walking Buddha and slender *chedi* shaped like a bell, and **Wat Trapang
Ngoen**, situated around a large lake which floods occasionally during the rainy season. Carry on to the west outside the
walled city and you reach **Wat Si Chum**, with its massive

seated Buddha measuring 15m (49ft) from knee to knee, and each finger the size of a person. The sanctuary walls are 3m (10ft) thick and contain a secret passage off to the left just inside the entrance. This passage was used by the king, though for what purpose is not clear.

The temple of **Wat Saphan Hin**, 2km (1 mile) west of the city, is known as the Temple of the Stone Bridge, after the slate pathway leading up the hill. It is a long haul to the summit, on which stands a Buddha statue more than 12m (40ft) tall. However, it is a trip that is well worth the effort.

Si Satchanalai

If you still have a craving for more temples, you may like to consider taking an afternoon's excursion to the city of **Si Satchanalai**, 55km (34 miles) to the north of Sukhothai. This is the sister city of Sukhothai, but is wilder and less visited by tourists, with ramshackle temples and an air of faded grandeur. At the top of a steep flight of steps is the ruined **Wat Khao Suwan Khiri**, which is worth the climb for the views alone.

Hire a bicycle from outside the historical park and explore what many regard as the city's most impressive temple, **Wat Chang Lom** (which translates literally as 'Temple Sur-

Loi Krathong

The best time of year to visit Sukhothai is on the full moon of the 12th lunar month (mid-November), when Thailand's most beautiful and serene festival, known as Loi Krathong, is celebrated. It is believed to have started some 700 years ago, after one of the king's concubines fashioned a lantern from carved fruit and sent it floating down the river bearing a lighted candle. Now, thousands of people gather by the lake to launch boats made of banana leaves and to marvel at the colourful processions of local women and a tremendous display of fireworks.

rounded by Elephants'). The *chedi* is surrounded by 39 standing elephants and has a stairway representing a ladder to heaven. Real elephants can usually be found in front of the temple, and it is often possible to get rides around the park.

In nearby **Ban Ko Noi**, a village 4km (2½ miles) to the north, archaeologists have discovered kilns that might revolutionise historical thinking by proving that the Thais began producing pottery 400 years earlier than the Chinese.

A row of Buddhas at Wat Phra Si Rattana Mahathat

Phitsanulok

A wide river cuts right through the heart of Phitsanulok, about 390km (240 miles) to the north of Bangkok, and separates the old part of town into two. Although the broad banks of the River Nan can make a pleasant spot to rest, the real attraction is **Wat Phra Si Rattana Mahathat**.

Believers have been coming here for centuries, praying in front of the renowned golden Chinarat Buddha, famous for its curative powers. The temple, with lovely mother-of-pearl doors from King Boromkot, was built in 1357, and its shrine is so popular that Thai tourists swarm here every day. To meet this demand, a variety of shops in the complex stock pendants, relics and other souvenirs. Apart from Wat Phra Si Rattana Mahathat, there are few reminders of the town's great history. A giant fire destroyed most of the old town several years ago, and now it is best known for comfortable hotels and as a base for Sukhothai excursions.

NORTHERN THAILAND

Stretching up to the borders with Myanmar (formerly Burma) and Laos, and following the line of the great Mekong River, northern Thailand incorporates some of the most beautiful scenery in the country. This region was once divided into small principalities, which were isolated by the rugged terrain and accessible only by elephant. Even today, the people of the region speak a distinctive dialect – influenced by Burmese and Laotian – and retain their own culinary specialities.

Getting there for today's visitor, however, is a simpler process than before. Thai Airways International flies to Chiang Mai in less than an hour from Bangkok, while air-conditioned express buses make the run in about nine hours, and overnight express trains in 12 to 14 hours. On a five-day visit, it is easily possible to explore the area around Chiang Mai and Chiang Rai – and even to take a trek among the northern hill tribes.

Chiang Mai

The capital of the north, **Chiang Mai**, rises from the banks of the Ping River, bedecked with dazzling flowers, notably orchid blossoms, in the spring. Formerly no more than a

Orchid Mania

Some of Thailand's remote areas are happy breeding grounds for over 1,300 different varieties of orchid, ranging from the famous *Paphiopedium ascocenda* to the elegant 'Miss Udorn Sunshine'. The best place to see them is at the orchid farms in the area around Chiang Mai, although you only need to look in markets throughout the country to see and appreciate the kingdom's favourite flower.

hillside Shangri-la, the town has grown rapidly to become both a tourist magnet and a major city in its own right – with the traffic and pollution to match. Several thousand luxury rooms and cheap, cheerful guesthouses are available, as well as European-style bars and restaurants. Tour operators offer countless trips to colourful handicraft villages, hillside temples and mountain tribes.

The orchid thrives around Chiang Mai

After the oppressive heat of Bangkok, the more temperate climate of Chiang Mai comes as a relief. The cooler weather is immediately evident (remember to pack a sweater if you are here between October and January), and so too is the abundance of fruit, vegetables and flowers, which can be seen at almost any time of year.

Chiang Mai means 'New Town' and was founded by King Mengrai the Great at the end of the 13th century *(see page 12)*. According to one legend, the city wall – parts of which can still be seen – was built by 90,000 men working in shifts round-the-clock. Mengrai also built various temples and fine buildings, some of which remain and can be explored on foot or by hiring a bicycle or motorbike. Don't forget to go to the handicraft centres nearby for silk, painted umbrellas and lacquerware.

Inside the City

Start your tour at **Wat Chiang Man** (open daily 9am–5pm), within the old city walls. Built in the 13th century under King Mengrai, it contains two important religious statues, the Crystal and Marble Buddhas – protected behind a railing, bars and glass – which were ancient long before this monastery had been conceived. Sculpted elephants surround a *chedi* at the rear of the temple.

Walk south for 15 minutes and you reach the huge, ruined *chedi* of **Wat Chedi Luang** (open daily 8am–6pm). Built in the 15th century, it was damaged during an earthquake over 400 years ago. In the temple grounds stands a gigantic gum tree shrouded in silk which, it is said, will continue to grow for as long as the city prospers. Beneath the tree, locals leave wooden elephants and phallic objects as offerings to the guardian spirit of the city.

Continue west to find **Wat Phra Singh** (open daily 8am–6pm), which is home to a magnificent Buddha statue. According to legend, the icon was on its way to the king when the chariot carrying it broke down in front of the temple. Believing this to be a signal that the image wished to go no further, the people installed it without question, and there

Wat Phra Singh's library is 1,000 years old

it has remained ever since, along with a beautiful library and several fine carvings and sculptures.

The best time of day to visit **Wat Suan Dok** (open daily 8am–6pm), which is off Suthep Road on the city outskirts, is at sunset, when the *chedi* is bathed in soft light. The ashes of the kings of Lanna are housed within the temple, which is said to hold an important relic of the Buddha.

Serene Buddhas adorn the many temples in the Chiang Mai area

A final temple not to miss is **Wat Jet Yot** (open daily 8am–6pm), also known as the Seven Peaks because of its seven *chedis*. Local guides say it was inspired by the great Mahabodhi Temple in India in 1455, during the reign of King Tilokaraja.

For visitors who want other forms of entertainment, Chiang Mai has plenty to offer. Drop in at the **Old Chiang Mai Cultural Centre** (open daily 7pm–9.30pm; admission fee is inclusive of dinner), which is in a charming old northern-style house, for traditional Lanna dance, dinner, and hill tribe demonstrations. Alternatively, you may wish to explore markets like **Somphet** (Moonmuang Road), or busy **Warorot** (Wichyanon Road), where you can try exquisite local delicacies. Finally, in the evening, make sure you don't miss the **Night Bazaar**, situated on Chang Klan Road, which offers a dazzling array of northern handicrafts. You'll be overwhelmed by the sheer variety, which is probably greater here than at any other market in Thailand.

Outside the City

Explore the following temples, villages and other attractions as part of either a half-day tour or a more extended itinerary. At the **Chiang Dao Elephant Training Centre** (open daily 8am–5pm; admission fee; tel: 0 5329 8553), 56km (35 miles) north from Chiang Mai, you can still see the vast creatures learning the arts of timber-lifting and bathing. Years ago, elephants were a common sight throughout the north, used for transport across inhospitable terrain and for dragging logs to the river, where they could be floated downstream. These days, elephants are the objects of more theatrical attention, with morning shows and river-washing staged for visitors. You can

Elephant camp at Chiang Dao

actually have a ride on one of the giants of the jungle, and then take a raft trip through the lush countryside, alive with colourful birds.

Wooden statues, huge clay pots and coloured paper umbrellas bedeck the road to the village of **San Kamphaeng**, 13km (8 miles) east of Chiang Mai, which is known as the handicrafts centre of northern Thailand. In the factories and warehouses, you can watch the locals as they weave silk from cocoons or make lacquerware or painted umbrellas. Afterwards, stock up on the best and brightest gifts in the kingdom. Purchases can be shipped home, and credit cards are widely accepted.

Some 16km (10 miles) northwest of Chiang Mai is the 1,600-m high (5,120-ft) peak of **Doi Suthep**. There are magnificent bird's eye views of the city and the surroundings from the summit and just below lies the most famous temple in North Thailand, **Wat Phra That Doi Suthep** (open daily). According to legend, during the 14th century a sacred white elephant sought out the site for the foundation of the temple by trumpeting three times and

Wat Phra That Doi Suthep

kneeling in homage to the Buddha. From the car park, it's a 300-step hike (or a comfortable funicular ride) to the central gold *chedi* at the top, with its royal bronze parasols at each corner. The cloister is lined with many important Buddha statues.

Continue another 4 km (2½ miles) past the temple to reach the **Phuping Palace** (gardens open only Fri–Sun and holidays 8.30am–4pm when the royal family is absent, admission fee), where the Thai king and queen often spend some of the winter. On weekends and holidays, if the royal family is not in residence, the grounds are opened to the public in a blaze of lavish floral displays.

Another attraction in the vicinity is the small Hmong or Meo village called **Doi Pui**. Since it is the most accessible of all Thailand's hill-tribe villages, you are unlikely to find much authenticity. Still, if you don't have time to go trekking, the village does give an idea of the hill tribes' way of life, and also includes a visit to the opium museum. Children sell colourful costumes, tassled bags and primitive handicrafts.

Among the Hill Tribes

To see the tribes in a more authentic environment, go along with an **organised trek** into the hills. You will probably have to walk considerable distances and sleep on less than luxurious floors, but with the aid of a guide, you can still locate numerous Karen tribes, who believe in the spirits of the winds and the rains, or the Lahu people, the men wearing silver buckles and black turbans and the women in calf-length tunics with yellow or white embroidery.

Known as the *chao doi*, the hill tribes are nomadic peoples who have migrated from Tibet and southern China along various routes into Burma, Thailand and Laos. In all, there are some 550,000 people, divided into six tribes: the Karen, Hmong, Akha, Mien, Lisu and Lahu, each with its own distinct dress, language and culture.

Generally, they are highland dwellers who opt to live above

Akha girls pose on the bridge to Burma at Mae Sai

1,000m (3,280ft). They earn a living from foraging, slash-and-burn agriculture and raising domestic livestock such as chickens and black pigs. All inter-tribal trade is done by barter. Traditionally, the *chao doi* have also shared a common mythology. They believe that they live on top of a dragon and that they have to keep the peace to ensure that it does not move.

Travel agencies in Chiang Mai operate excursions ranging from one-day trips to more rewarding three- and four-day expeditions. Don't expect too much originality, though – villagers may ask for payment for posing for photos. While some are friendly and seem to be pleased that their colourful bejewelled costumes and simple huts are a centre of attention, others have discarded just about every trace of their traditions, opting instead for jeans, T-shirts and cola.

Lamphun

Although legend has it that the most beautiful women in Thailand are from Lamphun, this is not the only reason for coming to this peaceful, ancient town, which can be found 30km (18 miles) south of Chiang Mai.

A large monastery in the town centre called **Wat Phra That Harlpunchai** is a busy educational and meditational institution. The huge, gold *chedi* in the middle of the monastery was begun over 1,000 years ago, and the workmen who erected it constructed their own simpler version outside the compound; it is now a ruin. Close by and built in modern style is the National Museum, which has a collection of sculptures

A typical limestone landscape in northern Thailand

found in the Lamphun district, dating from the 10th to 12th century.

You can take a pedicab from the centre of Lamphun to **Wat Chama Devi** (or Kukut), a temple that owes its existence to Queen Chama Devi, said to have founded it when she ruled the Mon kingdom of Lamphun well over 1,000 years ago. Of the original elements, most memorable is a *chedi* rising in five tiers with 60 standing Buddha images in stucco around the sides.

Look out for the *lamyai* orchards that have helped to make this region famous throughout Thailand. This delicious fruit, which is known as 'longan' in English, resembles a lychee.

Lampang

Don't be surprised if you see a horse and carriage trundling down the main road of this beautiful old town, 100km (62 miles) southeast of Chiang Mai – this is a common form of transport in Lampang, and the very best way to explore.

There are three temples here that deserve special mention. **Wat Phra Fang** has a tall, golden *chedi* with seven small shrines around the base. **Wat Phra Kaew Don Tao** reveals Burmese influence and has outstanding carvings. Considered by many to be northern Thailand's most attractive temple, **Wat Phra That Lampang Luang**, situated 18km (11 miles) from Lampang near the town of **Ko Kha**, is worth a visit for its museum and fine Buddha images.

Chiang Rai

Chiang Rai, a city 180km (111 miles) to the north of Chiang Mai, is mainly of use as a base from which to visit regional attractions, and you'll need to travel a short way out of town in order to see them. King Mengrai founded Chiang Rai in the 13th century, by chance so it is said. According to legend, his elephant ran off and took him to a spot on the Mae Kok River, where the scenery and military potential of the place inspired him to build a town. In recent years, town planners have made many improvements to the centre and river areas of the town.

There are at least two temples worth a visit. At **Wat Phra Kaew**, you can see a former home of the Emerald Buddha *(see page 26)*, the country's most famous image. At the Burmese-style **Wat Doi Chom Thong**, you have the bonus of views of the river below and a glimpse of the town's old quarter.

Travel agencies in Chiang Rai operate excursions to the famous hillside temple of **Doi Tung**, perched some 1,800m (5,904ft) up the mountain. On the way there you will pass the summer residence of Thailand's former Queen Mother, as well as an agricultural project sponsored by the Thai royal family designed to help hill tribes retain their distinctive traditions while integrating into contemporary life. The project encourages tribespeople to grow strawberries, cucumbers and cabbages, in lieu of opium. In return they receive

River ride

The most exciting way of arriving in Chiang Rai is not by the route through the hills, nor by the 45-minute flight, but by the least comfortable option of the riverboat from the town of Tha Ton. This is a trip for the adventurous – the boats are both small and narrow, with no toilets, while the engine is as loud (though not as powerful) as that of an aeroplane. Nonetheless, it is worth the effort – the views on the 4-hour journey are spectacular.

government assistance in the form of schools and new roads, plus income from tourists who come to purchase their wares.

Smaller tribal villages can also still be found in the mountains north of Chiang Rai and the area around **Mae Chan**. Be warned, however: pigs, water buffalo and dogs may still wander picturesquely among the stilt houses, but modern life has not passed by unnoticed, and the children will ask for coins or, increasingly, notes. Even among the Yao villages of adobe huts with thatched roofs, many elders have learned a few English words. The women, in red-collared jackets and blue turbans, are usually more interested in selling handicrafts than telling of the Yao's origins in southern China more than 200 years ago.

Mae Sai and Chiang Saen

You can't go further north in Thailand than **Mae Sai**; beyond is the footbridge across the Sai River into Myanmar (Burma). This charming little backwater with a sprinkling of markets and guesthouses is a good lunchtime spot on the way to the Golden Triangle. Get there between 6am and 6pm and you'll see authorised travellers from Myanmar crossing the border into Thailand to sell products such as cheroots, packaged prunes, ivory carvings, lacquer boxes, oranges and, more discreetly, items such as gems and contraband cigarettes. In the market, take your pick from the wonderful Burmese puppets and tapestries known as *kalaga*, or pay your 10 *baht* to photograph children dressed in hill-tribe costume. These days it's possible to cross the bridge and visit the Burmese border town of Tachileik, but occasionally it is closed for security reasons.

From Mae Sai, tours usually continue the 12km (7½ miles) to the infamous Golden Triangle, which forms a three-way border between Myanmar, Laos and Thailand. This spot, like many others, once saw huge quantities of opium being sent across the border, destined for heroin traders overseas. Now the figure is dropping, as a result of government encouragement to diversify into less sinister crops. Poppies won't be seen here, since discretion confines cultivation to the less accessible valleys, as well as to those vast areas in Myanmar that are controlled by the so-called 'opium armies'.

A short drive southeast from **Ban Sop Ruak** will bring you to the friendly town of **Chiang Saen**, set in a marvellous location on the banks of the mighty Mekong River. Despite its dilapidated feel, this town has a remarkably grand history. From the 10th to 13th centuries it was the seat of power for one of the earliest northern principalities – traces of this glorious past are scattered throughout this sleepy market town.

Rice cultivation – a common sight in Thailand

You can easily spend an afternoon exploring a moated city wall, the Wat Phra That Chom Kitti – reputed to house part of Lord Buddha's forehead – and the ruins of several other temples. Ten km (6 miles) north of Chiang Saen, the 5,600-sq m (60,280-sq ft) **Opium Exhibition Hall** (open Tues–Fri 8.30am–4pm; admission fee; tel: 0 5378 4444; <www.golden trianglepark.com>) uses high-tech interactive displays to chronicle 5,000 years of the use and abuse of opiates. Visitors who have more time for leisurely travelling may also be rewarded with beautiful sunsets over the Mekong, and marvellous views of Laos, just a stone's throw away.

Mae Hong Son

Wat Doi Kong Mu

December and January are the prime months to visit the town of **Mae Hong Son**, which lies squeezed between mountains 270km (167 miles) northwest of Chiang Mai and is reached by a hair-raising but staggeringly beautiful eight-hour road trip – or a less bumpy 30-minute flight. At this time of year, the sky is at its bluest, the winter flowers are in full blossom and the air is cool. It doesn't really matter which month you come, however, for this town offers no shortage of year-round attractions.

Until 1831, when an expedition was sent here by the king of Chiang Mai in search of the rare white elephant, Mae Hong Son's history was as misty as its valleys. The expedition was so successful that a small settlement was founded, and by 1874 Mae Hong Son had become a provincial capital.

Although you're unlikely to see wild elephants, you will come across a number Burmese-style temples around Mae Hong Son. They include **Wat Doi Kong Mu**, which looks down from the top of the 250-m (820-ft) high Doi Kong Mu, above the town, and affords views across the green Mae Hong Son valley and towards the neighbouring Shan state. Most people like exploring the market at dawn – when the hill-tribe people in traditional dress can sometimes be seen buying vegetables – before going on any one of a variety of tours. Guides arrange elephant-riding and river-rafting, or will drive you to tribal villages at the Burmese border.

Around Mae Hong Son you have the chance to explore caves and waterfalls. You may see the Padaung, or 'long-necked people', with their collarbones compressed by brass coils stacked up 30cm (1ft) high to make their necks appear longer than normal. Legend has it that the tribe's ancestors were a female dragon and the wind god, and it was in imitation of the image of the dragon that the women took up the unusual 'long-neck' tradition. Inevitably, the reality now is that this ungainly appearance is primarily designed to attract tourists.

On the return journey to Chiang Mai, while away a lazy day or more in the sleepy crossroads town of **Pai**. A firm favourite with backpackers, the valley hamlet is surrounded by mountains and is a good base for trekking.

On leaving Mae Hong Son, drivers and bus passengers could return to Chiang Mai on a circular route via Mae Sariang and Hot, so that towns visited previously are not repeated.

Dense jungle landscape on the road to Mae Hong Son

SOUTHERN THAILAND

Southern Thailand, stretching thinly down to Malaysia, gives you a choice of seas. The considerably longer eastern coast is on the Gulf of Thailand, while the west is washed by the Andaman Sea. On either side, though, you'll find sensational beaches, while the land in between – full of rice fields, and coconut and rubber plantations – is as scenic as it is fertile.

Planes fly to Phuket, Ko Samui, Krabi and Trang from Bangkok. Otherwise there are trains and buses, and the opportunity to explore several of the small, picturesque fishing villages along the way.

Phuket

The island of **Phuket** (pronounced 'poo-ket') is Thailand's top beach destination, with some of the most beautiful beaches and luxurious hotels in the land, in addition to sail-

Beach bums in Phuket

ing, snorkelling and nightlife. Covering around 810 sq km (313 sq miles) and made up of a mountainous interior, Phuket offers over a dozen white sand beaches, as well as national parks, inland plantations and waterfalls.

It attracts over 4 million tourists every year – almost 16 times the island's total population – most of whom arrive by plane (55 minutes from Bangkok), although tourist coaches also make the trip in just over 14 hours, crossing the causeway from the mainland.

Although Phuket has been transformed by the invasion of tourists, and new hotels are almost as abundant as water buffalo, you are nonetheless spoiled with some of the most beautiful scenery and clearest seas in the region.

Even historians might find something to interest them in Phuket. From the airport, the highway south goes through a dusty village called **Thalang**, the site of the island's ancient capital. Burmese invaders besieged, pillaged and destroyed Thalang in 1809. In an earlier and more positive chapter of history, the city managed to withstand a siege by the Burmese that went on for longer than a month. This battle, in 1785, led to both Lady Chan and her sister Lady Muk being regarded as heroines for taking command of the town's defence

Tsunami Disaster

On 26 December 2004, giant waves triggered by a powerful undersea earthquake just west of Sumatra crashed into coastal communities around the Indian Ocean. In southern Thailand, around 8,000 people perished, up to half of whom were foreign tourists, and many more were seriously injured. Some of the worst hit resort areas were Patong Beach on Phuket, Khao Lak north of Phuket and Phi Phi Island, but numerous simple fishing villages were also engulfed, creating an uncertain future for survivors whose livelihood depends on the sea.

following the death of Lady Chan's husband, the governor. Statues of these short-haired women warriors stand in a roundabout on the road.

The new capital, also called Phuket or **Phuket Town**, is not so much a sight in its own right as more of a departure and arrival point. A couple of streets of traditional two-storey Sino-Portuguese houses have been preserved, and a host of shopping centres, cafés and excellent seafood restaurants can be found. Souvenir shops sell wonderful seashells and locally cultivated – as well as counterfeit – pearls.

Most visitors, however, find it hard to tear themselves away from the sun and sea. Water sports of all kinds are offered, from waterskiing to paragliding, and windsurfers, catamarans and yachts can be hired. Fresh seafood makes for memorable meals, and everyone at some stage treats themselves to the famous Phuket lobster, which is best eaten grilled and with a dash of lime.

Beaches and Islands

The best beaches are on the western coast of the island, where fine, white sand slopes gently into the Andaman Sea (Indian Ocean). **Patong Beach**, 15km (9 miles) west of Phuket Town by paved road, used to be the island's most beautiful, but has become over-developed, packed with bungalows, hotels, restaurants, bars, pubs and discotheques. Despite having been hard hit by the tsunami, Patong beach has recovered significantly, and even the most heavily damaged places are now operational. From Patong, visitors can take a 45-minute longtail boat ride to **Freedom Beach**, which is located just around the headland.

At the wide beaches of **Kata** and **Karon** rapid building has provided an abundance of family resorts offering every comfort. More secluded is **Pansea**, home to the Amanpuri Hotel, one of the quietest and most exclusive addresses on the island

Ko Phi Phi beach

(see page 132). Further south at **Nai Harn** you will find one of the island's most sophisticated hideaways, Le Royal Méridien Hotel Phuket Yacht Club *(see page 133)* which is tucked into the cliff-side and affording marvellous views of the water.

It is possible to hire a Jeep in order to tour the island, but be warned that some roads are steep and accidents are not uncommon. The most dramatic viewpoint is the **Laem Promthep** promontory, which is 19km (12 miles) southwest of Phuket Town.

The sea views from Phuket are dotted with 30 or so uninhabited islands, to which owners of long-tailed boats operate excursions from some beaches for picnics and/or snorkelling. Scuba diving is first rate, with plenty of coral and brilliantly hued fish. Even better are the **Similan Islands**, which have National Marine Park status. Deep-sea fishing expeditions can be arranged to catch mackerel, barracuda and sailfish.

Excursions from Phuket

Phuket travel agencies offer a variety of day-long excursions. Anyone who knows the James Bond film *The Man with the Golden Gun* will not want to miss visiting the dramatic **Phang Nga Bay**, which contains the superb, mushroom-shaped rock formations featured in the film, and which still lure holidaymakers with their exotic appeal. Long-tailed boats skim through the mangrove into a dreamscape of mad mountain tops, and at two points of the journey sail through tunnels beneath limestone islands eroded by the tides.

On the way they will stop at **Ko Panyi**, where the Muslim fishing people have built a village on stilts above the sea and now enjoy the attention of thousands of tourists, who buy their woodwork and fresh fish. The real highlight, though, is **Ko Tapu** (literally 'Nail Island'), which was formed thousands of years ago as a result of an earthquake.

Phang Nga Bay, with its distinctive rock formations

The island rises straight up out of the water to a height of 200m (656ft).

A separate excursion is offered to **Ko Phi Phi**, which consists of two islands, Phi Phi Don and Phi Phi Leh. The larger of the two, Phi Phi Don, was devastated by the tsunami. Reconstruction

Island escapes

Adventurers can escape the crowds by hiring boats to more distant, uninhabited islands – just make sure that before leaving you agree on the price and the number of islands that you will be visiting.

is taking place, and it is likely that some areas on the island will be re-designated as a park. Boats go from Phuket daily and the trip south lasts two hours. Day tours will take you to the Viking Cave and to beautiful Maya Bay. Do spend a night there if possible, so you will have time to enjoy some of the most incredible scenery in the country. Underwater enthusiasts can explore some of the richest marine life to be found in the Andaman Sea. Fish are not the only attraction either, for high up in the sea cliffs live a vast number of sea swallows. The nests that the birds build so industriously at great heights are collected at considerable risk to the islanders – it's a profitable export business, supplying Chinese restaurants with the raw material for that expensive delicacy of bird's-nest soup. Locals believe that the soup will cure skin and lung problems as well as impotence and loss of appetite. Such is the demand that some nests fetch prices as high as US$1,000 each.

Closer to Phuket – and considerably cheaper – is the popular **Naga Pearl Farm** (open daily 9am–3.30pm; admission fee; tel: 0 7742 3272), which can be visited by a half-day excursion to Naga Noi Island. This is home to the biggest cultivated pearl in the world, weighing a massive 30 gm (1 oz). Boats carry groups of tourists to the island daily to watch the pearl cultivation, and after lunch will drop you back at your hotel.

Ko Samui

Backpackers long ago thought that they could keep **Ko Samui** secret. However, this palm-fringed island, just three hours from the busy seaport town of Surat Thani, has become one of the best-known havens in the south, with idyllic hotels and bungalows and even an airport. Not that it has necessarily spoilt the laid-back feel of the place, for people are still coming here to laze on the beaches, eat excellent seafood, and be pampered at one of the sumptuous spas that have sprung up all over the island.

Honeymooners and comfort seekers often stay on **Chaweng Beach**, which is arguably the most beautiful stretch, packed with restaurants and discos. If you want something more chilled, head to **Bo Phut**, **Maenam** and **Choeng Mon** beaches. For cheaper hotels and bungalows, head for the south.

If you feel like doing more than just catching the rays, a host of beach sports is offered, as well as tennis, waterfall trips and even an excursion to a coconut-picking farm. For an afternoon diversion, you can also hire a motorcycle or Jeep to tour the island. The road follows the coast almost all the way round, though you should stop off at **Lamai** to take photographs of the erotic rock formations known to all as 'grandfather' and 'grandmother' rocks. Remember that the roads here are steep – and tourists with grazed knees are by no means an uncommon sight. A safer means of transport on the island is a *songthaew* (covered pickup truck with seats), which run almost 24 hours.

Getting there

There are daily flights from Bangkok to Ko Samui, taking just 50 minutes. Buses take 15 hours (including the ferry crossing), while trains run to Surat Thani, from where it is 2 hours by boat to Ko Samui.

Ko Samui has a host of beach and water sports

Beyond Samui

Samui is the largest island in an archipelago of 80 islands that also includes the party haven of Ko Pha Ngan, the dive mecca of Ko Tao, and the stunning uninhabited ruggedness of Ang Thong National Marine Park. Ferries and speed boats shuttle visitors daily between the various shorelines, with Ko Pha-Ngan the closest and quickest to get to.

Geared more toward backpackers than luxe travellers, **Ko Phangan** is best known for its legendary **Full Moon Party** on **Hat Rin** beach. Attracting thousands of ravers each month, the party is synonymous with drug taking, and while the local authorities have made some effort to stem the rampant narco-consumption, most revellers euphorically dance the night away on cloud nine.

Far more tranquil is a day tour of the 40 wild islets and lagoons that comprise the beautiful **Ang Thong National**

Marine Park, which inspired the fictitious island paradise in Alex Garland's novel *The Beach*. Further north is **Ko Tao** (Turtle Island), a small and pretty island with a relaxed atmosphere. Most visitors here come to experience the quality dive sites, with the numerous dive shops here being the island's mainstay.

Hat Yai

More than two-thirds of the way down the southern coast, and half an hour's drive inland, you will come to a town best known for sex and smuggling. **Hat Yai** is the fastest-growing provincial capital in the country, and as such has to deal with the crowds of Malaysians who cross the border daily for cheap shopping and sin.

The ongoing unrest between the Thai government and Muslim separatists in the southern provinces of Yala,

The Loi Krathong Festival in Hat Yai *(see also page 56)*

Narathiwat and Pattani, has also occasionally spilled over (with deadly results) to Hat Yai district. While travelling here is still generally safe, check the latest reports and advisories for the region before venturing to the deep south.

Songkhla

Although **Songkhla** has never been known for its nightlife, this sleepy town – which is situated 30km (18 miles) northeast of Hat Yai and is the very antithesis of its neighbour – offers a wide range of other attractions, among them lakes, beaches and grand ramparts. It is quiet, dignified, and has a colourful history.

> ### Bird sanctuary
>
> Ornithologists will want to see one of southern Thailand's greatest bird sanctuaries, the Khu Khut Waterfowl Park. Occupying 520 sq km (200 sq miles) of the Great Songkhla Lake, the park hosts some 140 resident and migratory species. The best way to see them is by hiring a long-tailed boat. Try to go during the early morning or late afternoon – when the birds are at their best – to avoid being roasted by the heat.

Even though the white sand beaches here go on for miles, swimming is not good and the season is short. It's better to walk along the shady waterfront or to lunch at the outdoor seafood restaurants. On the eastern side of the peninsula, where Thailand's biggest lake meets the sea, the port of Songkhla is as colourful as its red, blue and green trawlers. You can watch these landing giant prawns, and then follow the seafood to market. For cultural interest, try the National Museum, which is over a century old and houses collections of local archaeological finds, old furniture, and items from the prehistoric site of Ban Chiang. Parts of the old fort, with 18 turrets, can also be seen on Red Mountain.

WHAT TO DO

Thailand offers an unbeatable choice of indoor and outdoor activities, even if the heat is such that sometimes all you want is a swim. If you find you're lucky enough to be in Thailand at the time of a major festival, make sure that you don't miss one of the country's most joyous occasions.

SHOPPING

From the moment you reach Thailand you'll be astounded by a wealth of things to buy. Locally made items range from stunning silk products to wooden bowls and silver earrings, from silk textiles and clothing to fine woodwork and fragile, colourful pots. Whatever you are looking for you will find in **Bangkok**. **Sukhumvit Road** is crammed with large, modern shopping malls and department stores where there is no shortage of either imported or local offerings.

Nor is Bangkok the only option. **Chiang Mai** is renowned for its handicrafts, while even the smaller towns in the northeast of the country offer many of their own specialities. In **Phuket**, the main Airport–Phuket highway has a good selection of handicrafts and Chaweng at Samui is awash in typical tourist gear.

Remember that bargaining is the rule just about everywhere, apart from supermarkets and hotels – with even the large, upmarket boutiques occasionally being amenable to a little bit of negotiation. But do keep in mind that fixed-price shops may sometimes be no more expensive, and they come with the added bonus of some form of guarantee. A word of caution: only buy jewellery from reputable shops.

Colourful Thai silk (see pages 88–9)

Chiang Mai's famous Night Bazaar

Markets and Bazaars

Air-conditioned shops might sound like the best idea in the big cities, but it is the local markets that offer the real bargains. They are definitely worth a visit, if only to see the crowds and experience the excitement. Don't forget to bring a camera and to get there early, since many are like ghost towns by the middle of the day.

One of the most famous markets in Thailand is Chiang Mai's **Night Bazaar** *(see page 61)* where you can find quality silks, handicrafts, rugs and clothing for sale, among many other items. The market gets going at dusk and the vendors start packing up just before midnight.

In the capital there are several markets worth a visit. One of the biggest, most diverse and best-known markets in Bangkok is the **Chatuchak Weekend Market** *(see page 35)*. Fruit, vegetables and spices all vie for space with food concoctions you've probably never come across before. As for take-home curios, you might like a brass temple bell, a carved buffalo horn, a hill-tribe embroidered garment, or some handmade silver jewellery. You'll also find a huge selection of vintage and trendy street-style clothing, rare antiques, funky home ware and furnishings, plants and pets.

A relative newcomer and with an uncertain future, **Suan Lum Night Bazaar** across from Lumphini Park, is a well laid out and less frenetic alternative to the weekend market. Aimed at tourists, stalls of handicrafts, clothing, souvenirs and the like jostle among beer gardens and restaurants.

The weekday equivalent of Chatuchak can be found at the Thieves' Market, Pahurat and Chinatown, all located within easy reach of one another.

Chinatown is worth a visit simply for the sightseeing. The emphasis here is on goods with a Chinese flavour or origin. The **Thieves' Market** has a wide range of curios, some of them antique – but remember that you need an export certificate for genuine items *(see page 112)*.

For sumptuous silks, clothing, cloth and delicate batiks, some real bargains are to be found in **Pahurat** market. Here, products from as far away as India and Malaysia are sold alongside local items.

The Art of Bargaining

Want a natty wooden elephant, a lurid leather bag or even a ride in a *tuk-tuk*? Then remember to bargain for it. First ask how much the price is. Then name a figure considerably lower and somewhat less than you are prepared to pay, and eventually aim to meet up in the middle. A few hints to help out: always check the prices on several stalls to get an idea of the real cost; don't be misled by sweet smiles and sob stories – and remember, at the end of the day, so long as you are happy with the price you've got a bargain.

Images of Buddha

Taking images of Buddha or other deities out of Thailand is prohibited, and the export of antiques is strictly controlled.

Best Buys

Antiques. If you qualify as an informed collector, then you'll find worthwhile objects from Thailand, Myanmar, China, Laos and Cambodia at the Thieves' Market, in smarter shops or in the provinces. Experts at the National Museum in Bangkok meet the public on both Sundays and Mondays, when they vouch for the authenticity of works of art and antiquity. Export permission is required for taking genuine antiques or art treasures out of the country (see page 112).

Art. Paintings in several media by Thai artists, usually on familiar rice paddy or temple-spire themes, are sold in galleries and shops all over the main towns. Temple stone rubbings on rice paper are another typical souvenir.

Bronze. A great Thai tradition, bronze is now used for tableware in addition to lamps, bells, candelabra and statues.

CDs and DVDs. While Thailand has made some effort to stamp out pirated music, movies and software, many market stalls still warily offer all the latest media releases. Buy at your own discretion.

Ceramics. A particular wood is used in the kilns to fire celadon, a distinctive Asian form of pottery with a delicate green glaze. Porcelain is also made in Thailand. Ming and Ching dynasty bowls and shards turn up, salvaged from the river at Ayutthaya and Sukhothai.

Fashion. Clothes to order – allegedly in 24 hours or less – can be a bargain, but try to give the tailor several days if you want a first-rate garment. Trousers, dresses, suits, shirts and bikinis can all be made to measure. Women's ready-to-wear shops often sell good cheap copies of current European fashions. The domestic fashion industry is also coming into its own, with lots of trendy boutiques in Bangkok malls and around Siam Square.

Tribal crafts include miniature figures carved from wood

Furniture. Rattan and hardwood furniture pieces are often bargains and can be made to order. Bangkok and Chiang Mai have the best selections. With the ongoing success of teak farming and teak recycling, teak furniture has once again become a bargain in Thailand if you find the right places. Asian rosewood is also a good buy.

Gems. Precious stones such as sapphires and rubies are mined here, while others are imported at favourable prices from Myanmar (Burma), India, Sri Lanka and other countries. Bangkok claims to be the world's top gem-cutting centre. Seek out a reputable shop and avoid unrealistic bargains: fakes are common.

Handicrafts. With great skill, patience and ingenuity, the artisans of Thailand produce an apparently endless variety of hand-crafted objects. Each region has its specialities.

Homeware. Contemporary Thai design has become extremely creative in recent years, with many designers infusing traditional crafts and materials with ultra-modern twists.

Jewellery. Thai designers tend towards traditional styles, but original designs can be ordered. Choose carefully where you shop: the establishments that cater to tour buses are generally more expensive because they often pay the travel agency a 20 percent kickback on what you spend. Thai costume jewellery can be a great bargain.

Lacquerware. Look out for pretty gold-and-black boxes in the shape of fantasy animals.

Nielloware. Black metal alloy inlaid on silver is an ancient craft now deployed on jewellery and trinkets.

Pottery. A typical Thai variety – *benjarong* ware – has a five-coloured design on a background of grey, white or black. You will also see patterned porcelain jars, plates and pots.

Thai silk and fabrics. Happy silkworms keep thousands of nimble weavers busy, hand and foot, in producing the famous, colourful Thai fabrics. Ranging from lightweight

Hand-painted parasols are made by locals around Chiang Mai

blouses to heavy bedspreads, the long-lasting fabrics live up to their worldwide reputation. Durable Thai cotton, most of which is factory-made, goes into ready-to-wear clothing, towels, some toys and tablecloths. Keep an eye open for brightly coloured padded jackets.

Umbrellas. All around Chiang Mai, locals make hand-painted parasols – to your own design, if you wish.

Wood carvings. Figurines, elephants and hippos, teak furniture, salad bowls and a variety of other knick-knacks are exquisitely carved from wood.

ENTERTAINMENT

Thai Dance, Dance-drama and Music

The highly stylised classical *khon* drama, based on the *Ramayana* epic, was performed solely at royal palaces for the privileged. In a *khon* performance, masks are donned for all roles except the three leads where heavy make-up and ornate costumes subdue the personality of the performers. The modern adaptations presented during dance shows are generally known as *lakhon* where no masks are worn and the movements are less stylised. The *lakhon chakri* is often performed at temple festivals and at shrines. The popular burlesque theatre, known as *likay*, is much coarser, and is interspersed with slapstick episodes. The entertaining transvestite shows always include several *likay*-type scenes. The shadow theatre known as *nang thalung* originated in the south of the country and is staged against a backlit white cloth screen. It is most commonly performed in South Thailand.

Classical Thai music can sound like a mishmash of contrasting tones without any pattern. To aficionados, it has a very distinct rhythm and plan. A classical *phipat* orchestra is made up of a single reed instrument, the oboe-like *phinai*, and a variety of percussion instruments.

Apart from the Erawan Shrine, the only places to view traditional dance and theatre in Bangkok are a few restaurants which host dinner shows. One troupe that is struggling to survive is the **Joe Louis Puppet Theatre** (tel: 0 2252 9683) at the Suan Lum Night Bazaar in Bangkok, which stages a *hun lakhon lek* puppet show every evening at 7.30pm.

Nightlife

Mention Bangkok to anybody and the chances are they will talk about the city's nightlife. In recent years the city has welcomed a whole slew of stylish bars and clubs that are slowly helping the capital to distance itself from its salacious reputation. Lounge bars, fabulous roof-top bars and chic design-conscious clubs are all the rage now. Quality music has at last become a must, with bars hosting weekly DJ-driven theme nights and also pulling in big name international DJs.

The government's implementation of the Social Order Campaign in 2001, which was meant to clamp down on rampant drug abuse and under-age drinking, means that no matter how old you are, some nightlife venues are now forced to turn away anyone who does not hold identification, be it an ID card for locals, or passports for international

Thai dancers at the Erawan Shrine in Bangkok

visitors and residents. There are occasional drug raids by the police, and all official nightspots are currently forced to close between 1–2am (depending on the area).

Nightclub-style restaurants specialise in traditional Thai food and music, with performances by Thai dancers or regional folklore. Otherwise, cultural possibilities suitable for foreign visitors are quite limited. Visiting musicians sometimes perform, as do local theatre groups. Most cinemas show the latest Hollywood offerings. The Thai film industry has recently come of age with a few productions even making it in the West, the best example being *Suriyothai*, an epic concerning the history of Ayutthaya.

The Go-Go Scene

In just Bangkok alone you can choose from several hundred nightclubs and go-go bars, and throughout the country several thousand more. These, along with the thousands of escorts and dancers who work in them, cater to every taste. Although they are obviously aimed at single, heterosexual males, women are usually welcome to come in for a drink and a look. Gay bars are increasingly run in the same areas, particularly in Bangkok and Chiang Mai.

In Patpong – usually seen as the best-known red-light area of the lot (more people visit it every year than the Grand Palace) – there are even markets, pizza shops and Thai boxing displays for entertainment.

Before you go, remember a few words of warning. Upstairs 'bars' are frequently a front for live sex shows and you may find yourself faced with a very large bill for your drinks. It is wise always to check the price before entering any Patpong bar. If there is trouble, simply pay the bill and get in touch with the tourist police. Don't accept the advice of touts (including taxi drivers) who try to tempt you to visit live sex shows and other pornographic diversions. Remember too that go-go bar 'women' are not all female, and that Aids and venereal diseases are common.

Provincial nightlife is often calmer than that in the capital, though many towns have nightclubs with hostesses for hire, massage parlours and the like. Pattaya has a comprehensive nightlife comparable with Bangkok's. Down in the far south, Phuket outdoes all other seaside tourist towns with a highly concentrated entertainment zone in Patong Beach.

SPORTS

With some of the most beautiful waters in the Far East, it's little wonder that Thailand is a beach-lover's paradise. Once you have finished sunning yourself, there is no shortage of other activities. Boats and windsurfers are available for hire at beaches, as are pedal boats and speedy little jet skis.

Thai boxing combines punching with kicking

Fishing has only been exploited recently as a sport in Thailand, but now Bang Saray has become something of the 'headquarters', although good catches of sailfish, marlin and shark have been made by several fishing specialists in Pattaya. But if all you want is a day relaxing on deck with a rod to tempt snapper, mackerel or parrotfish, that can easily be arranged as well.

Exploring the waters of Phang Nga Bay

Scuba diving is especially good around Ko Tao and similar islands, but is available at most of the major resorts, and lessons are also offered. If you want to get really serious, you can progress from beginner to internationally certified undersea diver in five days of training. **Water-skiing** fans will find the required equipment and powerful boats at popular beaches. Away from the water,

Spectator Sports

The most popular spectator sport in Thailand is undoubtedly football and many Thais watch the games on television. It is Thai boxing (*muay thai*), however, that is most unusual for the visitor. This unique – if violent – sport combines Western boxing with Eastern martial arts. As well as using gloved fists, these agile punchers and kickers battle it out with their elbows, knees and feet. Fights are held year-round at Lumphini and Ratchadamnoen stadiums in Bangkok and at festivals and fairs around the country.

golf has taken over Thailand. Hua Hin is a very good destination for golfers wishing to play on championship courses.

Trekking in the northern mountains is becoming increasingly popular. Week-long treks usually include three meals a day and basic camping equipment. The best town from which to begin a trekking tour is Mae Hong Son, where countless tour agencies offer trips with licensed guides.

CHILDREN'S ACTIVITIES

Thailand is not an ideal destination for children. They may not take to the heat well, and few really enjoy visiting temples or taking in Thai architecture. Of all the destinations in Thailand, Chiang Mai offers the best range of activities for children. At the **Maesa Elephant Camp** (open daily 8am–4pm; admission fee; tel: 0 5320 6247; <www.maesaelephantcamp.com>) at Km 10, Maerim-Samoeng Road, Maerim District, 30km (19 miles) from the city, kids can learn about and ride on elephants. The **Thai Buffalo Training Camp** (open daily 8am–5pm; tel: 0 5330 1628), at 300/2 Muang Pha Huay Zai Road, Rimneua, offers a chance to see a race between five water buffalo – after they've demonstrated the ploughing of a rice field.

In action at the Buffalo Training Camp

Most families with children choose a beach holiday in southern Thailand. Some resorts offer some children's activities, such as supervised games in the swimming pool, while others do not allow children below a certain age. Check with your hotel when booking.

Calendar of Events

Check precise dates before you leave as the timing of many festivals and events depends on the position of the sun or the moon.

Late January–early February Chinese New Year. Many Thais have Chinese ancestry, and this week-long Lunar New Year festival is always celebrated with much gusto.

February full moon Makha Puja. A nationwide Buddhist festival with candlelight processions around many temples.

Early February Flower carnival in Chiang Mai, with floats, parades and beauty contests.

13–15 April Songkran or Water Festival. Thai New Year is celebrated nationwide by throwing water at everybody in sight.

Early May Visaka Puja. This very important Buddhist holiday commemorates the Buddha with candlelight processions.

May The Royal Ploughing Ceremony in Bangkok. Just before the rainy season starts, the king presides over ceremonies to bring good rains to farmers.

May Bun Bang Fai (rocket) festival in the northeast. Fireworks light the sky to bring rain.

July full moon Asanha Puja. Candlelight processions at every temple in Thailand to celebrate Buddha's first sermon.

12 August Queen's Birthday. Also known as Mother's Day; this is a public holiday.

Early October Phuket Vegetarian Festival in Phuket Town. Chinese festival with male penitents piercing their bodies with knives and needles.

November full moon Thailand's most beautiful festival, Loy Krathong. Thais across the country launch small candle-laden floats on rivers and lakes *(see page 56)*.

Late November River Kwai Historical Week in Kanchanaburi. A week-long festival to commemorate the events of World War II with memorial services and a sound-and-light show over the famous bridge.

5 December The king's birthday is celebrated in Bangkok with an elaborate parade on Ratchadamnoen Klang Avenue.

EATING OUT

Good food in Thailand is as ubiquitous as beaches – and often quite a lot hotter besides. If you don't like chillies, don't give up on the food. *Mai phet* (not hot), stressed at the time you order, can bring a delicious selection of cooler, more subtle flavours that may include any taste from the sweetness of coconut milk to the pungency of fresh lemon grass, garlic or nutmeg and the saltiness of fermented fish. Added to that are tropical fruits such as fresh pineapple, a little sugar, a pinch of coriander – and, of course, a lashing of culinary inspiration.

Busy in the kitchen

Every region has its own gastronomical specialities. Up in the north, a local sausage known as *naem* is popular. The northeast is famed for its *khao niaw* (sticky or glutinous rice), normally served as an accompaniment to barbecued meat, as well as *som tam*, a tasty hot salad that combines shredded green papaya with dried shrimp or curried crab claws, lemon juice, garlic, fish sauce and chillies. The south produces numerous dishes that have been influenced by the Muslim style of cooking of the Malays and, of course, all kinds of seafood dishes, including crab, squid, shark, freshly cooked lobster and mussels. Don't worry if you have a sweet tooth – you're not likely to go hungry at all. Many Thai sweets are based on rice flour, coconut milk, palm sugar and sticky rice, and just about all of them are delicious.

When and How to Eat

Most Thais work all day, grab something quick for lunch and have an early dinner. But don't think that the Thai version of fast food is just a bland rice dish. A 'quick bite' often means a tasty dish (such as *pad thai*) of sautéed noodles with pork, shrimp or chicken and seasoned with tamarind juice, lime, basil, garlic and onion. Even breakfast for locals consists of dishes full of fresh herbs and spices, such as sweet curry soup with basil served with boiled rice noodles. Hotels rarely serve such traditional Thai breakfasts although they will direct you to a nearby restaurant that offers them.

Food vendors line the streets everywhere and sometimes it may seem as if everybody is eating or drinking at all hours. Local markets teem with vendors selling food items such as nuts, dried meats and sweets. If you're feeling adventurous,

Street Fare

On the whole, the best and certainly the cheapest meals will be found at food stalls which line the streets. Housewives buy their ingredients fresh and inexpensively at the market in the early morning and prepare their best dishes. There are usually no menus as each stall offers a few specialities. Buying from food stalls poses no language difficulties, as you simply point at what you want. The food stalls may look rather dubious, but remember that unlike restaurants, everything is prepared before your very eyes. Westerners who have spent some time in Thailand have complete faith in these streetside stalls.

skip the hotel breakfast and stroll through an open-air market sampling the various treats. At lunch it'll be too hot to have the Thai soups so opt for a salad and noodle dish. Plan on having your main meal in the early evening, just after sunset when the temperature drops.

Soup is traditionally eaten throughout the meal. If you are a newcomer to Thai food, start off with something mild and then maybe work up to pig's intestine soup or chilli-flavoured serpents' heads! Also good to start with are curries *(kaeng phet)* – particularly those with a coconut-cream base, which are less piquant than Indian curries – and there is never any shortage of wonderful, tasty fresh fish. There is no need to hold back on quantity or restrict yourself to one dish. Thais will usually order a selection and share them as a group.

When eating chillies, take a local tip and have plenty of steamed rice, which helps to soothe the stomach and will

Typical Thai fare

smother the fire. Nothing else is as effective, and cold drinks are the worst antidote possible – they just make it worse.

Thai restaurants often welcome customers with cold, and even sometimes frozen, hand towels, as a relief from the tropical world outside. Many restaurants have also taken to issuing disposable mini-towels in small plastic packets; the explosions you hear all about you are the Thais smacking the air-tight packs to open them.

Don't expect to find knives on Thai tables – a spoon is used instead. Sauces will be offered that you can use to season your dish instead of salt and pepper. One of them is *nam pla*, a salty caramel-coloured fish sauce with tiny chilli segments in it. *Nam phrik*, 'pepper water', is a much-prized concoction of pounded red chillies, shrimp paste, black pepper, garlic and onions mixed with tamarind, lemon juice, ginger and fish in an early state of fermentation.

Small bowls of roasted chillies are also served on the side for diners with a more robust constitution – from the famous *phrik kee noo* ('mouse-dropping pepper') to the potent *phrik chii faa*.

What to Eat

Appetisers. *Paw pia tawt* is a Thai spring roll enclosing sweet-and-sour bean sprouts, pork and crabmeat. *Gai hor bai toey* consists of chicken chunks fried with sesame oil, soya sauce, oyster sauce, herbs and a drop of whisky, all in a leaf wrapper. *Krathong thong* are delicate mouth-size patty shells filled with a delicious combination of minced chicken, sweetcorn, carrots and soy sauce.

Soup. *Tom yam* is a hot-sour soup, made with either pork, shrimp, chicken or fish, which must be accompanied by plenty of steamed rice to soak up the excess chilli heat. *Kaeng jeud* is a less pungent soup made from chicken, pork and shrimp cooked with Chinese-style vegetables, glass noodles and Thai herbs and spices. *Tom kha gai* is a spicy chicken soup with coconut milk and lemongrass. *Bah mee nam* is a rich broth of thin noodles, pork or chicken chunks, mixed with herbs, bean sprouts and subtle spices.

International Fare

For a change of both taste and scenery, try one of the various Asian restaurants that serve a spectrum of different cuisines – almost all of them at bargain prices. By far the most common non-Thai Asian cuisine is Chinese food. In Bangkok you can sample the most important regional schools of Chinese cooking – Szechuanese, Cantonese, Shanghainese and Pekingese – as well as the less familiar food of the Hakka, Chiu Chow and Hunan peoples.

Restaurants specialising in food from neighbouring Cambodia, Malaysia, Burma and Laos are not easy to find, but Japanese, Korean and Vietnamese food is well-represented.

The significant population of Thais of Indian descent or Muslim religion accounts for the availability of curries and associated foods. Indian food per se is not prevalent in Thailand but in Bangkok there are several restaurants to choose from. In Bangkok some of the luxury hotels offer surprisingly good Italian food.

In the upmarket shopping malls (such as Emporium) you'll find several trendy cafés and restaurants serving a fusion of Eastern and Western cuisine. There are also a plethora of fine Italian eateries throughout the city, and you will find French bistros, English pub fare, steak and rib joints – and even the odd Mexican – quite easily.

Crispy fried prawns and other favourites

Rice and noodles. *Kao pad* is fried rice with bits of meat. *Mee grob* is crispy fried rice noodles with pork, egg, bean sprouts, shrimp, and a sweet-and-sour flavour. *Pad thai* is served many different ways, but is basically flat dried rice-flour noodles sautéed with garlic, onion, tamarind juice and a variety of spices, and served with vegetables.

Seafood. *Hor mok pla* is a fish curry with vegetables and coconut milk, served wrapped in banana leaves. *Pla preow wan* is fried fish covered in a thick sweet-and-sour sauce. *Gung tod* – or crispy fried prawns – usually comes with a choice of sauces. *Pla samlee daet deow* is a whole deep-fried cotton-fish traditionally served with a tangy mango salad.

Chicken and meat. *Gaeng mud-sa-man* is a beef curry – less spicy than most – and has an overtone of peanuts. *Kao nah gai* is sliced chicken with spring onion, bamboo shoots and steamed rice. *Sa lad neua san* translates as roast beef salad and contains vegetables, chillies, garlic and perhaps mint. *Kaeng ped gai naw mai* is red chicken curry with bamboo shoots, lime and basil leaves. *Kaeng ped* is roast duck curry, sometimes served with slices of fried aubergine.

Sweets. *Salim* is a refreshing sweet of sugared noodles with coconut milk and crushed ice. Ice cream, pronounced 'eye-cream', sometimes comes in original and natural flavours. A local variation of a sundae, for instance, is coconut ice cream sprinkled with peanuts and kernels of corn. *Khao tom mad* is sticky rice with coconut cream and bananas.

Fruit. *Somo* is a pomelo, a tropical cousin of the grapefruit, and is served divided into sections. *Sap-pa-rot*, or pineapple, is a familiar fruit but twice as tasty on its home ground. More exotic local fruits are rarely on restaurant menus, but can be discovered at markets and street stalls. Just point if

A selection of fruit

you don't know the name. *Ngor* (rambutan) looks like a hairy and overdeveloped strawberry; the fruit is inside. *Lamut*, a light-brown fruit that has to be peeled, is syrupy sweet, with a taste reminiscent of fresh figs. *Durian*, that green monster with spiky thorns, contains bits of custard-like fruit around egg-shaped piths. Its smell is often compared to

Popular local brand of beer

that of a rubbish tip, although its creamy interior is deliciously sweet and luscious. Try local oranges, bananas, mangoes, papayas – almost every fruit imaginable, except apples and pears, which don't grow here and are expensive.

What to Drink

Iced water is frequently served at the start of a meal. It's almost bound to be safe to drink in any decent restaurant, but if in doubt ask for a bottle of water and skip the ice *(see page 116)*. Thais usually drink water or cold tea *(cha jin yen)* throughout their meal, along with beer or whisky with dinner.

Because of high import duty, wines are very expensive in Thailand. Even in a modest restaurant, an undistinguished wine could cost more than the whole dinner. Thailand does produce good beer, though: brand names to try are Singha, Kloster and Chang – all stronger than you might expect.

Thai whisky, on the other hand, is weaker and cheaper than you'd think: Mekhong is the best-known brand, though too much can result in a frighteningly bad hangover.

To Help You Order

Could we have a table?   **Kor toh dai mai?**
I'd like a/an/some...   **Chan yak dai ...**

beer	**beer**	milk	**nom**
beef	**neua**	noodles	**kwaytio**
bread	**khanom-pang**	pork	**moo**
chicken	**kai**	rice	**kao**
coffee	**kafae**	salt	**kleua**
curry	**kaeng**	shrimp	**kung**
egg	**khai**	soup	**soop**
fish	**pla**	sugar	**nam tan**
meat	**neua**	tea	**cha**
menu	**maynu/**	water	**nam**
	raigarn arharn	wine	**low wai**

Some basic ingredients

HANDY TRAVEL TIPS

An A–Z Summary of Practical Information

A

ACCOMMODATION

The balance between supply and demand in Bangkok and the major tourist destinations varies enormously, but advance reservations for hotel rooms are always a good idea. Always request the promotional rates when booking. Bangkok has one of the world's least expensive hotel rates for luxury hotel rooms. Many of these promotional rates include a full breakfast and sometimes also include limousine transfers from/to the airport. Booking your hotel through a tour operator or at a local travel agency is the best way to get the bargain rates and packages. The busiest months nationwide are November to February. Outside the high season, especially in the resort destinations, bargain room rates are to be had.

Bangkok has a plethora of rooms considered suitable for foreign tourists; budget travellers will find many no-frills, native-style hotels as well. Of the former, even the cheapest are completely air-conditioned, and many have swimming pools and other comforts. Almost all hotel rooms in the country come with a private bathroom. International-standard hotels are also found in the regional capitals such as Chiang Mai and Hat Yai. High-end hotels normally charge a standard 10 percent service and 7 percent VAT to the room, so always check if the rate is includes the additional 17 percent fees.

At the beach destinations of Phuket and Ko Samui there are world-class resorts that tend to be rather expensive when compared to Bangkok or Chiang Mai. Note that May and June are the slowest months at these resorts, with Phuket being especially tourist-free in May, when even lower than off-season rates may be found. Breakfast is sometimes included in the rates; be sure to ask at check-in. In smaller towns, facilities may be fairly basic – but so are prices.

| Do you have a (double) room? | **Mee hong (kuu) mai?** |

AIRPORTS

Air service to Bangkok is excellent with non-stop flights arriving daily from London, Sydney, the US, many European, and most Asian cities. **Suvarnabhumi** (pronounced 'su-wan-na-poom') **Airport** (call centre tel: 0 2132 1888; <www.airportthai.co.th>), also known as **New Bangkok International Airport (NBIA)**, opened in September 2006. Approximately 30km (19 miles) east of the city, this airport has the largest terminal and the tallest control tower in the world. Thailand has five other international airports: Chiang Mai, Hat Yai, Phuket, Samui and Sukhothai.

Depending on the time of day, immigration queues can be long and slow. In the arrival hall excellent facilities, including porters, limousine service, hotel desks and a Tourism Authority of Thailand (TAT) information office, are available 24 hours a day. Free local telephone calls can be made from call boxes in the arrival and departure halls.

Air-conditioned taxis are available from the counter outside the arrival hall. Tell the desk clerk your destination and this will be written in Thai on a slip and handed to the driver. Make sure the driver turns on the meter. There will be an airport surcharge of 50 *baht*. If you have agreed to use the expressway for a quicker journey, there will be an extra 60 *baht* in toll fees. The trip from the airport to Bangkok's hotels takes about 40 minutes, depending on the traffic. Expect to pay about 200–300 *baht* to get to the city centre.

If you're flying on **Thai Airways International** (THAI; <www.thaiair.com>) from your originating city to your final destination within Thailand, you may not have to clear customs in Bangkok. Ask at check-in where your bags need to be collected.

Domestic flights are fairly inexpensive and THAI is the principal carrier to Phuket, Chiang Mai, Chiang Rai and Mae Hong Son, among others. The arrival of low-cost airlines has brought down the cost of domestic travel. These include **PB Air** (<www.pbair.com>), **Nok Air** (<www.nokair.com>), **Air Asia** (<www.airasia.com>) and **Orient Thai** (<www.orient-thai.com>). **Bangkok Airways** (<www.

bangkokair.com>) is your only choice if you're heading to Ko Samui. Those heading for Pattaya can take an air-conditioned coach there directly from the airport (about 1 hour).

In March 2007 the old **Don Muang** airport, 23km (14 miles) north of Bangkok, reopened. A large number of domestic services have relocated there from Suvarnabhumi. These include many of THAI's flights, plus all domestic flights of Nok Air and Orient Thai.

Chiang Mai International Airport (CNX; tel: 0 5327 0222 for information) is located just 15 minutes from the city centre. From **Phuket International Airport** (HKT; tel: 0 7632 7230 for information) the journey to most of the resorts takes 30 to 45 minutes. **Ko Samui Airport** (USM; tel: 0 7742 5012 for information) is just 5km (3 miles) from Chaweng Beach. Taxis are available at all domestic airports. Be sure to settle on the rate before heading out. Almost all the deluxe hotels in Thailand offer round-trip airport transfer at a fixed rate (usually quoted in US dollars). Request this convenient service when making your reservations.

B

BICYCLE AND MOPED HIRE

Although cycling is not advisable in the horrors of Bangkok's traffic, bikes can be rented at several hotels and guesthouses. At beach resorts such as Pattaya, Ko Samui and Phuket, bikes and mopeds can be hired through your hotel reception or travel counter. Chiang Mai lends itself to exploration by bike or moped and some resort hotels, such as The Regent, offer guests free bicycle use.

BUDGETING FOR YOUR TRIP

Bangkok is inexpensive when compared to most major cities. After you budget for airline tickets and hotels, you can spend as little as 500 *baht* per day on meals and still eat very well. There are approximately 68 *baht* to 1 pound, 36 *baht* to the US dollar.

Transport. Taxi: 100–400 *baht*.

Metro, SkyTrain 10–40 *baht* per trip.

Average fare of a domestic one-way flight: 2,500 *baht*.

Average fare of a domestic rail ticket to other provinces: 500 *baht*.

Average fare of a domestic bus ticket to other provinces (air-conditioning on bus): 300 *baht*.

Average *tuk-tuk* fare: 20–100 *baht*.

Meals. Dining at the deluxe hotels is considerably more expensive than at local restaurants. On average, breakfast and lunch will cost around 250 *baht* at simple restaurants to 500 *baht* at the expensive hotels. A top-class dinner will cost 1,000 *baht* per person in Bangkok or at the resort destinations. A better-than-average dinner will cost around 600 *baht* and a very good dinner will cost around 300 *baht*. Wine is very expensive in Thailand.

C

CAMPING

Several national parks offer camping facilities, as do a number of the islands. Camping is not recommended outside in the wilds, as robberies and hold-ups are not uncommon. Contact the local TAT office to get detailed information on campsites and rates *(see page 126)*.

CAR HIRE (See also DRIVING)

Most travellers do not hire a car when visiting Thailand. Driving is stressful and the roads are not easy to navigate.

Budget and Avis offer car hire throughout Thailand.

Budget tel: 0 2203 9200; <www.budget.co.th>.

Avis tel: 0 2251 1131; <www.avisthailand.com>.

Local companies may be less expensive but are often less reliable and not likely to offer roadside assistance if you encounter a problem. Expect to pay between 1,600 and 2,400 *baht* per day for a small car; and between 2,800 and 5,000 *baht* for a large saloon car or mini-van.

Always opt for the full insurance package, especially the Collision Damage Waiver (CDW). Although some credit card companies cover this, you'd have to produce an enormous amount of paperwork that would be difficult – and costly – to translate from Thai.

CLIMATE

Thailand enjoys its best weather just when the northern temperate zone is suffering the worst of winter. November to February are the favoured months in Bangkok, ironically known as the 'cool season', when the temperature dips a bit below the usual debilitating extreme and, more important, the humidity is lower. Rain is quite rare.

The following chart for Bangkok gives the average maximum and minimum daily temperatures and number of rainy days per month:

Although temperatures of 36–38°C (97°–100°F) are common in the hot season, widespread use of air-conditioning relieves the discomfort. The rainy season (monsoon) lasts from about May to October. It rains mostly in the afternoon or evening, cooling and refreshing the tropical air, and inundating the streets.

	J	F	M	A	M	J	J	A	S	O	N	D
av. max. (°F)	89	91	93	95	93	91	90	90	89	88	87	87
av. max. (°C)	32	33	34	35	34	33	32	32	32	31	31	31
av. min. (°F)	68	72	75	77	77	76	76	76	76	75	72	68
av. min. (°C)	20	22	24	25	25	25	24	24	24	24	22	20
rainy days	2	2	4	5	14	16	19	21	23	17	7	1

CLOTHING

Pack for the tropics; cotton is preferable. A light sweater might come in handy if you are planning a trip to the hills during the winter; the only other place you may feel cold is in an air-conditioned restaurant.

Immodesty should be avoided: adults should not wear shorts when visiting temples, and women with plunging necklines will receive plenty of stares, not all admiring. The Thais are strict about covering up, except on the beach, but are quite casual as regards dressing up – even the Grand Palace no longer requires jackets and ties (but shorts and tank tops are not welcome). Almost all restaurants and nightclubs share the same informal approach.

COMPLAINTS (See also POLICE)

If you have a dispute with a hotel, merchant or any organisation or person in Thailand, it is important not to lose your temper. If your complaint has no effect after you have tried approaching the person or establishment concerned directly, consult the Tourism Authority of Thailand *(see page 126)*. In serious cases, the tourist police can often be of assistance in resolving the problem. From anywhere in the country dial 1155 from any phone (including pay-phones). You'll get an English-speaking operator in Bangkok who will locate the nearest Tourist Police officer to your location.

CRIME AND SAFETY (See also EMERGENCIES)

Beware of pickpockets in crowded marketplaces. Bag-snatchers speed away on a motorbike almost before the victim realises what's happened. Don't tempt bandits by flaunting jewels or ostentatious clothes, and always use the safety boxes that come free of charge with many hotel rooms. Alternatively, deposit your valuables at the hotel's main safety box, but always obtain a receipt.

At seaside resorts, never leave any valuables on the beach when you go swimming. At Phuket, the authorities advise tourists to avoid isolated beaches, where they might be accosted by robbers.

CUSTOMS AND ENTRY REQUIREMENTS

For a visit not exceeding 30 days, visitors from many countries, including the UK and US, do not need a visa to enter Thailand, just a passport valid for at least 6 months, and a return or onward ticket. Visas can usually be extended by up to 10 days at immigration offices throughout the country. If you plan to stay more than a month, obtain a 60-day visa at a Thai consulate or embassy in your country before leaving home. Check <www.thaivisa.com> or the the websites of Thailand's immigration <www.immigration.go.th> and the Ministry of Foreign Affairs <www.mfa.go.th> for details.

Currency restrictions. There is no restriction on the import of foreign currency, but amounts over the equivalent of 10,000 US dollars must be declared. On leaving the country, you may take out up to 10,000 US dollars or the equivalent in foreign currency (more if declared on arrival).

When leaving Thailand, note that the export of any images of Buddha or other deities is prohibited. The export of antiquities without special permission from the Fine Arts Department is also prohibited. Some shops will be able to handle this for you, or you can contact the office directly: National Museum, Fine Arts Department, 4 Na Phra That Road, Bangkok, tel: 0 2224 1370.

D

DRIVING

Road conditions. As in many Asian countries, traffic in Thailand is supposed to keep to the left. Due to chronic traffic jams, driving conditions in the Bangkok metropolis are appalling. Peak traffic persists almost all day, with only brief periods of respite. On the main highways out of town, free-spirited drivers make up their own rules as they go along, using whatever part of the road they feel they need, even if it means running another car into a ditch. As you discover the local driving customs, you won't need reminding to stay extremely alert. Watch out, too, for buses in one-way streets going in the opposite direction to traffic.

Rules and regulations. An International Driver's Licence is required for visitors. The official speed limit is 50km/h (30mph) in towns, 80km/h (50mph) on main roads, 90km/h (56mph) on motorways.

Fuel. Readily available in both regular and super; petrol stations are now closing before 10pm as an energy-saving measure.

Parking. Parking bays are found on some streets.

If you need help. Telephone the agency from which you rented the car to come and rescue you. In an emergency dial the Highway Police Patrol Centre, tel: 1193.

Road signs. Most road signs are in English. Speed limits are always posted in Arabic numerals.

accident	**u-bat-fi-het**
collision	**rot chon**
flat tyre	**yang baen**
Help!	**chuey duey!**
Police!	**tam ruat!**

E

ELECTRICITY

The standard current in Thailand is 220-volt, 50-cycle AC; most hotel rooms have an electrical outlet for shavers; some have 110-volt sockets, too. Plugs are two-pin and you'll need adaptors (and transformers depending on where you're coming from).

EMBASSIES AND CONSULATES

Australia: 37 Sathorn Tai Road, Bangkok, tel: 0 2344 6300.

Canada: 990 Rama IV Road, Abdulrahim Place, 15th Floor, Bangkok, tel: 0 2636 0540.

Ireland: 28th Floor, Q. House Lumpini Building, 1 Sathorn Tai Road, tel: 0 2677 7500.

New Zealand: All Seasons Place, 87 Wireless Road, Bangkok, tel: 0 2254 2530.

UK: 14 Wireless Road, Bangkok, tel: 0 23053 8333.

US: 120–122 Wireless Road, Bangkok, tel: 0 2205 4000.

EMERGENCIES

In case of an emergency dial **191**. For less dire emergencies, contact the Tourist Police on 1155.

G

GAY AND LESBIAN TRAVELLERS

Due to its tolerant Buddhist culture, there is little discrimination against gays and lesbians in Thailand. There are no gay movements since there is little anti-gay sentiment in the country. Public display of affection, however, is frowned upon. In Bangkok, Chiang Mai and Phuket there are several gay-owned establishments such as bars, restaurants and small hotels.

For more information, contact Utopia, a gay and lesbian cultural and information centre in Bangkok, tel: 0 2238 3227. Purple Dragon is a highly respected company that provides travel services for gay and lesbian travellers. More information can be obtained at <www.purpledragon.com>.

GETTING THERE

Air travel. Suvarnabhumi Airport *(see AIRPORTS)* is the principal gateway to Thailand and a major airport of entry to the Far East. There are non-stop flights from many major cities including London, Auckland and Sydney. Flights from the US West Coast all stop either in Hong Kong, Tokyo or Osaka. There is a very frequent service (almost hourly) from Singapore, Kuala Lumpur and Hong Kong.

International airports. Phuket is the second gateway to Thailand with non-stop flights arriving from Perth, Hong Kong and Singapore. The airports at Chiang Mai and on Ko Samui are also served non-stop from Singapore for those visitors wishing to by-pass Bangkok.

Rail travel. Comfortable trains run from Singapore to Bangkok, including the luxury service run by the Venice-Simplon Orient Express, known as the Eastern and Oriental Express.

GUIDES AND TOURS

Avoid unauthorised guides who greet you on the street and offer to show you Bangkok. In Bangkok and, to a lesser extent, in the larger provincial towns of Thailand, touts, black marketeers and pimps often pester tourists. Some are charmingly convincing, others obnoxiously persistent. The best course is to smile and walk away.

Contact the Tourism Authority of Thailand (TAT) for a list of licensed English-speaking guides in the region you wish to visit. Licensed guides are required by law to wear their official photo-identification card around their necks at all times. There are no set rates even with these licensed guides, so decide on where you want to go, what you want to do and negotiate the price accordingly. The guide will usually sit next to the driver in a private car or a small mini-bus and take you where you want to go.

Rates vary enormously. The best way to calculate a fair price is to find out how much a group guided tour costs and offer double that price for a private guide. Group tour information is available at all TAT offices *(see page 126)*, or you can ask your hotel receptionist to get an idea of the rates. If you're happy with your guide and driver, it is customary to invite them to eat with you, or pay for their meal, especially if you are on the road all day. Alternatively, you may tip both the guide and the driver at the end of the day.

Guided boat tours are a pleasant way to see Bangkok's river and canals – enquire at your hotel for details. For cheap, do-it-yourself sightseeing, take the Chao Phraya River Express boats *(see page 35)* for an hour's trip up or down the Chao Phraya; fares range between 9–32 *baht*. Longtail boat taxis ply the narrow inner canals and cost between 5–10 *baht*, depending on distance. Piers are located near traffic bridges. The main downtown artery begins at Tha Saphan Phanfah near Wat Saket, goes through downtown Bangkok, and ends at Bang Kapi. For exploring the canals of Thonburi and Nonthaburi, private longtail boats can be rented from most of the river's main piers. Rates should be negotiated beforehand, and these cost

500–700 *baht* for 1 hour for the entire boat, and rising to 900 *baht* for 2 hours. Each boat can seat up to 16 persons.

H

HEALTH AND MEDICAL CARE

No vaccinations are required to enter Thailand.

Never drink the tap water anywhere in the country. Bottled water is readily available everywhere. Responsible restaurants serve bottled water and pure ice, but be cautious about the ice in drinks at roadside stands. To be on the safe side in questionable situations, insist on bottled water or soft drinks and beer without ice.

Many Westerners suffer some kind of intestinal discomfort from the spicy food, the excessive heat and the unusual ingredients. Spare your digestive system by experimenting gradually until you're more accustomed to the Thai cuisine. Avoiding fresh vegetables and unpeeled fruit is a good idea except at the top hotels and restaurants and don't eat uncooked foods at market stalls.

Most major hospitals in Thailand accept credit cards. Hospitals are of the highest standards in Bangkok and there's always a pharmacy open 24 hours. Prices for medical services are significantly below equivalent charges in Europe and the US. Pharmacies nationwide are well-equipped and can dispense over the counter many medications that require prescriptions in Western countries.

a bottle of drinking water	**nam yen nung khuad**
I need a doctor	**pom/chan tong karn maw**
I need a dentist	**pom/chan tong karn maw fan**

HOLIDAYS / FESTIVALS

Since many Thai holidays and festivals are fixed to the lunar calendar, the dates vary from year to year. Banks and government offices are closed on these days, but daily life is not necessarily disrupted. The only notable exception to this is Chinese New Year, which is not a public holiday in Thailand, but a time when most businesses are nevertheless closed.

1 January	New Year's Day
6 April	Chakri Day, honouring Rama I
13–15 April	Songkran (Water Festival)
1 May	Labour Day
5 May	Coronation Day
12 August	HM the Queen's Birthday
23 October	Chulalongkorn Day, honouring Rama V
5 December	HM the King's Birthday and National Day
10 December	Constitution Day
31 December	New Year's Eve

Variable dates
Chinese New Year (1st month of the lunar calendar, usually Jan/Feb).
Maka Puja (full moon in February). Commemoration of meeting at which the Buddha preached the doctrines of Buddhism.
Visakha Puja (full moon in May). Celebrates the birth, enlightenment and death of the Buddha. Most holy Buddhist ceremonial day.
Asanha Puja (full moon in July). Celebrates Buddha's first sermon.

L

LANGUAGE

Although English is widely used in hotels and shops and is the best-known Western language in Thailand, try to use some simple phrases in Thai. The Thai language spoken in Bangkok is understood everywhere in the country, though there are many dialects and sub-dialects. Like Chinese, Thai uses intonation to distinguish between otherwise identical words, which makes it a difficult language for foreigners. Each syllable can have up to five different meanings depending on how it is pronounced; there are 44 consonants plus dozens of vowels, compounds and tone marks. If all this doesn't discourage you, consider Rachasap, a special language used only when speaking to or about Thai royalty!

Try to imitate a Thai to learn how to intone useful words; your efforts will be appreciated by everyone you meet. You will find a brief list of useful expressions on the front cover flap of this guide, as well as those listed below.

SOME USEFUL EXPRESSIONS
Numbers

one	**neung**	fifteen	**sip-har**
two	**sorng**	sixteen	**sip-hok**
three	**sarm**	seventeen	**sip-jet**
four	**see**	eighteen	**sip-(b)paet**
five	**har**	nineteen	**sip-gao**
six	**hok**	twenty	**yee-sip**
seven	**jet**	thirty	**sarm-sip**
eight	**(b)paet**	forty	**see-sip**
nine	**gao**	fifty	**har-sip**
ten	**sip**	sixty	**hok-sip**
eleven	**sip-eht**	seventy	**jet-sip**
twelve	**sip-sorng**	eighty	**(b)paet-sip**
thirteen	**sip-sarm**	ninety	**gao-sip**
fourteen	**sip-see**	one hundred	**roy**

Days of the Week

Monday	**wan jan**	Friday	**wan suk**
Tuesday	**wan ang karn**	Saturday	**wan sow**
Wednesday	**wan put**	Sunday	**wan ar tit**
Thursday	**wan pa ru hat**		

thank you	korp khun kap (if you are a man)
	ka (if you are a woman)
hello/goodbye	sawatdee kap (if you are a man)
	ka (if you are a woman)
yesterday	mua wan nee
today	wan nee
tomorrow	prung nee
day/week	wan/sap da
month/year	duan/(b)pee
left/right	sai/khwa
up/down	bon/lang
good/bad	dee/lehw
big/small	yai/lek
cheap/expensive	took/phaeng
hot/cold	rorn/yen
old/new	gao/mai
early/late	chao/sai
easy/difficult	ngai/yark
heavy/light	nak/bao
here/there	tee nee/tee nan
next/last	nar/tee laiw
quick/slow	rehw/char
When does ... open/ close?	... pert/pit meua rai?
What's the fare to ...?	(b)pai ... kit thao rai?
stop here	jop teenee
turn right	lieo khwa
turn left	lieo sai
Could you speak more slowly?	Poot char long dai mai?
I don't understand	mal kao chai
I'm sorry/excuse me	kor thort

LAUNDRY AND DRY CLEANING

Many hotels will take care of your laundry for you, returning it within 24 hours and even within four hours at premium rates. Dry cleaning takes two days unless 'express service' is specified, when it takes half the time but costs 50 percent extra. There are some semi-self-service launderettes in Thailand where you can drop off a load of laundry, place it in the washing machine and it will be dried and folded for you at roughly 30–50 *baht* per kilo. This service is considerably less expensive than hotel laundry services which usually charge 50–100 *baht* per item. More self-service machines are appearing outside corner shops on residential *sois* across Bangkok.

M

MAPS

The Tourism Authority of Thailand *(see page 126)* issues free bus and tourist maps showing the principal attractions of Bangkok. These aren't always adequate, though, and it is better to buy one of the commercially produced maps of Bangkok and Thailand that are sold at hotels and bookshops. Interesting specialised maps of the waterways and markets of Bangkok are also available. For quirkiness, check out Groovy Maps and Nancy Chandler's maps.

MEDIA

The *Bangkok Post* and *The Nation* are Thailand's leading English-language newspapers. They are available at most hotels and airports and are updated daily online at <www.bangkokpost.com> and <www.nationmultimedia.com>.

There are five terrestrial Bangkok TV channels, and many programmes are foreign shows, mostly American, which are dubbed into Thai. Most leading hotels provide satellite TV channels which usually include CNN and the BBC world news services 24 hours a day.

Bangkok's English-language radio stations can be found on 95.5FM and 105FM. These stations offer music interspersed with hourly news bulletins and weather reports.

MONEY

Currency. The unit of currency in Thailand is the *baht* (abbreviated THB, Bt or B), divided into 100 *satang*. Banknotes come in denominations of 20, 50, 100, 500 and 1,000 *baht*. Coins are 25 and 50 *satang*, and 1, 5 and 10 *baht*.

Banks and exchange facilities. Normally the exchange rate at banks is the most favourable. After the banks are closed you can change money at your hotel, at exchange booths or at shops displaying a sign in English saying 'money changer'.

Banks and money-changers in tourist towns will accept virtually any currency.

Credit cards. Major hotels, restaurants and shops are accustomed to the well-known international charge cards. Small eateries and small shops tend to accept cash only.

ATMs. Facilities for using your debit or credit card to withdraw money automatically are widely available in Thailand, especially in Bangkok and at the major airports.

OPENING HOURS

Business hours are 8.30am–noon and 1–4.30pm, Monday–Friday for government offices. Banks are open 8.30am–3.30pm. Department stores are usually open 10am–10pm seven days a week. Hours are extended just before Christmas, New Year and Chinese New Year. In seaside tourist areas, many shops are open from early in the morning until 11pm or even midnight during the high season. Note that state-run museums are closed on Monday and Tuesday.

P

POLICE

A special force of Thai Tourist Police operates in crucial areas of Bangkok and throughout the country, such as near tourist attractions and major hotels. The officers, all of whom speak passable English, stand ready to protect or advise foreigners. They wear the beige military-style uniform of ordinary Thai police, but with 'Tourist Police' shoulder patches. Dial 1155 from any phone in the country to reach the Tourist Police.

POST OFFICES

Bangkok's main post office is open 8am–8pm Monday–Friday, 8am–6pm, Saturday and Sunday. Branch offices are usually open 8am–4.30pm, Monday–Friday, 9am–noon on Saturday. Branch offices are scattered throughout the country and can also be found at the airports.

You can send letters and postcards airmail, which should arrive within five days to a week in Europe or North America. Almost all the big hotels offer basic postal services, and many newspaper shops sell stamps.

PUBLIC TRANSPORT

Metro. Bangkok's mass transit system, also called the subway, is an underground network that supplements the existing Skytrain service, and passengers can transfer between the two networks at three interchange stations. Both the Metro and Skytrain provide the most efficient way of navigating the city in air-conditioned comfort and speed. Fares start at 14 *baht*, increasing 2 *baht* every station, with a maximum fare of 36 *baht*. Tourists may find it more convenient to buy the unlimited-ride 1-day pass (150 *baht*), 3-day pass (300 *baht*), or the stored-value Adult Card (200 *baht*, including a 50 *baht* deposit), depending on their needs. The subway operates 5am–midnight.

Skytrain. The elevated mass transit system, as with the Metro, is fast, frequent, clean and comfortable. Single-trip fares are between 10 and 40 *baht*. Tourists may purchase the unlimited-ride 1-day pass (100 *baht*), or the 30-day pass (which comes in three types: 250 *baht*, 10 rides; 300 *baht*, 15 rides; 540 *baht*, 30 rides), or the stored-value Adult Card (200 *baht*, including 50 *baht* deposit); these are available at all station counters. Trains run 6am–midnight.

Buses. Buses are slower but much less expensive, averaging just 6 *baht* in Bangkok. A well-developed network of city buses serves other cities too. Fares are low and service is as good as can be expected in a traffic-jammed metropolis. If you plan to cut your expenses by using buses instead of taxis, you may find it useful to buy one of the Bangkok street maps which shows the routes. All city buses have route numbers marked in Arabic numerals, but destinations are written in Thai.

Inter-city coaches range from rickety veterans to comfortable air-conditioned cruisers, and prices vary accordingly. On the heavily travelled routes, like Bangkok to Pattaya, luxury coaches operated by various companies make frequent departures.

Trains. Thailand's state railway system <www.railway.co.th> provides an efficient means of seeing the country. There are reasonably luxurious air-conditioned first-class carriages, comfortable second-class accommodation (including couchettes, which can be reserved) and old-fashioned, wooden third-class carriages. Travel agents, hotel desks and the information office at the main (Hualamphong) railway station can advise you on timetables and fares. Bangkok's main stations are:

Hualamphong on Rama IV Road – for the north, east and northeast and for express trains to the south.

Thonburi on Bangkok Noi, Rod Fai Road – for the slower trains to the south.

For general information on rail travel, tel: 1690.

Taxis. In Bangkok, taxis are abundant. They are metered, air-conditioned and inexpensive (35–80 *baht* average). They can be hailed anywhere along the streets. To avoid a hassle, ask your hotel receptionist to write down your destination in Thai script, which you can show to the driver. The hotel receptionist should also be able to advise you what the appropriate fare will be; this depends on the distance and the traffic.

If you can't stand the language problem, you can take an air-conditioned hotel taxi. The fares are set, and are usually at least twice what a public taxi would cost, but they have the advantage that drivers very often speak some English.

Tuk-Tuks. Useful and adventurous for short trips, these noisy little three-wheeled motorbikes nip in and out of Bangkok's traffic; they're also readily available in Chiang Mai and Phuket and convenient if you're just trying to get from the beach back to your hotel.

R

RELIGION

In Thailand, more than 90 percent of the population are Theravada Buddhists, but other faiths are well represented, including Islam (especially in southern Thailand), Christian, Hindu and various animistic religions (especially in northern Thailand).

T

TELEPHONES

Thailand's country code is 66. To make an overseas phone call from Thailand you must first dial 001 followed by the country code and area code. If you need international call assistance, dial 100. To avoid hotel surcharges on phone calls, call from one of the public telephones located in post offices throughout the country. Some of them offer a 24-hour international service. Rates (usually per minute with a 3-minute minimum) are posted in English.

Prepaid international phone cards can also be used for making international calls. These can be bought at post offices or the office of the Communications Authority of Thailand (tel: 0-2950 3712).

Mobile phones. Only users of GSM 900 or 1800 with international roaming facility can hook up automatically to the local Thai network. Check with your service provider if you are not sure. An alternative is to buy a local SIM card with a stored value from a mobile phone shop. This will have a local number, and local calls made to and from the phone will be charged at local rates.

TIME DIFFERENCES

Thailand time is GMT plus 7 hours throughout the year. When it's noon in Bangkok in winter, it's 9pm the day before in Vancouver and Los Angeles, midnight in Toronto and New York, 5am in Dublin and London, 7am in Johannesburg, 4pm in Sydney and 6pm in Auckland.

TIPPING

While tipping is not the norm for Thais, it is more prevalent in Bangkok, Pattaya and Phuket than in other parts of Thailand. Tip taxi drivers 10 percent; hotel maids 20 *baht* per day; porters 20 *baht*; tourist guides 15 percent; restaurant staff and bartenders 10 percent; massage therapists 10 percent; hairdressers 10 percent.

TOILETS

Try to find a hotel or restaurant. In luxury establishments the toilets are spotless. Away from the main centres, you will encounter hole-in-the-floor toilets. In places without running water, you will always find a huge jar of water nearby. Scoop water out for flushing and washing. Toilets are free.

Where are the toilets?   **Hong nam yu tee nai?**

TOURIST INFORMATION

The **Tourism Authority of Thailand (TAT)** runs information stands in the arrivals hall of the Suvarnabhumi Airport and at Chiang Mai and Phuket airports.

You can also obtain leaflets, maps and advice at the organisation's head office: 1600 New Phetburi Road, Makkasan, Ratchathewi, Bangkok 10310; open daily 8.30am–4.30pm, tel: 0 2250 5500, <www.tourismthailand.org>.

Branch offices of TAT are located in Chiang Mai, Kanchanaburi, Nakhon Ratchasima (Korat), Pattaya, Hat Yai, Ko Samui and Phuket. All branches have useful regional information and maps. In Chiang Mai the address is: 105/1 Chiang Mai-Lamphun Road, tel: 0 5324 8604.

Overseas representatives of the Tourism Authority of Thailand can be found in the following countries:

Australia: 75 Pitt Street, Royal Exchange Building, 2nd floor, Sydney 2000, tel: 61-2-9247 7549.
UK: 98–99 Jermyn Street, London SWIY, 6EE, tel: 020-7925 2511.
US: 611 North Larchmont Boulevard, Los Angeles, CA 90004, tel: 1-323-461 9814; 61 Broadway, Suite 2810, New York, NY 10006, tel : 1-212-432 0433.

W

WEBSITES

<www.tourismthailand.org> The official site of the Tourism Authority of Thailand with information on all aspects of travel in Thailand.
<www.thaiair.com> The site of the state-run airline, Thai Airways International, with timetable, fare and availability details for all flights to Thailand, as well as domestic flights.
<www.bangkokair.com> Timetable and fare information for all Bangkok Airways flights to Ko Samui and other destinations.

<www.asiatravel.com> Information on all aspects of travel to and within Thailand, including hotels and museums.

<www.hotelthailand.com> This site is an excellent resource for detailed hotel information throughout the country, especially those hotels offering special discounts and incentives.

<www.circleofasia.com> Provides maps, photos and guides to Thailand's different regions, plus reliable hotel and tour bookings.

<www.phuket.com> The site contains all the details of this seaside resort and surrounding areas.

<www.sawadee.com> A good resource for detailed information on tourist attractions in Thailand.

<www.bangkokpost.com> The internet version of the daily English-language newspaper is a good site to obtain up-to-the-minute local news and weather reports as well as listings of current cultural events. Its travel archives are also an excellent resource on finding discounted hotel and travel packages for travel within Thailand.

<www.untamed-travel.com> Online version of the popular travel and listings magazine.

WEIGHTS AND MEASURES

You're unlikely to come across anything other than the metric system when you go shopping. The exception to this is the measurement used to describe the weight of gold, which still uses the old Thai system (1 *baht* = 15.16gm). Though Thailand turned metric in 1923, traditional units of length (1 *sauk* = 0.5m; 1 *wah* = 2m; 1 *sen* = 40m) and area (1 *rai* = 1 sq *sen*) still survive.

Y

YOUTH HOSTELS

Thailand has youth hostels in Bangkok, Chiang Mai and Phuket. Refer to *Hostelling International*, published by the International Youth Hostel Federation, or <www.iyhf.org> for more details.

Recommended Hotels

Luxury hotels in Bangkok are among the world's least expensive and most travellers take advantage of the many promotional rates offered at the city's world-class establishments. It is imperative to make advance reservations for the high season, from December to March, especially for the resort destinations of Phuket and Ko Samui. During the low season, from April to October, there are almost always rooms to be had. The Tourist Authority of Thailand (TAT) has airport and city-centre offices in all major destinations; many are open seven days a week, to assist travellers who arrive without reservations. All hotels are air-conditioned. A 7 percent Value Added Tax (VAT) and 10 percent service charge is added to hotel bills and, unless noted below, all hotels accept major credit cards. Published, or 'rack' rates, may be high at the hotels listed below, but always ask for promotional rates which offer up to 60 percent savings. Reservations made through tour operators or through the TAT will also normally ensure a lower price than the hotel's rack rates. And always check the hotel's website (where available) as many hotels offer 'internet-only' rates at substantial savings.

$$$$	over US$200
$$$	US$125–200
$$	US$80–125
$	less than US$80

BANGKOK

Holiday Inn Silom $$ *981 Silom Road, Bangrak, Bangkok 10500, tel: 0 2238 4300, fax: 0 2385289, <www.bangkok-silom. holiday-inn.com>*. Located right next to the Jewellery Trade Centre towards the river end of Silom Road, this comfortable hotel is of much higher quality than its Holiday Inn branding would suggest. It is only an 8-minute walk to Surasak Skytrain station. 700 rooms.

Intercontinental Bangkok $$$ *973 Ploenchit Road, Bangkok 10330, tel: 0 2656 0444, fax: 0 2656 0555, <www.bangkok.inter*

continental.com>. For off-river accommodation in the heart of the shopping district, steps from Chit Lom Skytrain station, this hotel is an excellent choice. Extensively renovated in 2004, the deluxe rooms are spacious with large sound-proofed windows overlooking the bustling city. There are three restaurants, a pool, health club, spa and a beauty salon. 381 rooms.

Old Bangkok Inn $ *609 Phra Sumen Road, Phra Nakhon, Bangkok 10200, tel: 0 2629 1785, <www.oldbangkokinn.com>*. Located within stone's throw of Bangkok's major historical landmarks, this personable boutique inn is recommended for its beautifully decorated guest rooms, modern amenities, as well as friendly and knowledgeable service. 8 rooms.

The Oriental $$$$ *48 Oriental Avenue, Bangkok 10500, tel: 0 2659 9000, fax: 0 2659 9284, <www.mandarin-oriental.com/ bangkok>*. More than 130 years old, the world-renowned Oriental Hotel is Bangkok's longest-established luxury hotel. All the rooms are plush, with special touches such as hardwood floors in the bathrooms. As well as the Oriental Spa, there's a Thai cooking school, three of the city's best restaurants, two swimming pools and a health club. Afternoon tea is served in the Authors' Lounge, named after the many famous writers who have stayed at the hotel. 395 rooms.

Park Avenue Hotel $ *30 Sukhumvit Soi 22, Bangkok 10110, tel: 0 2262 0000, fax: 0 2258 2328, <www.hotelparkavenue.com>*. The main shopping district of Sukhumvit, including the Emporium shopping complex, is just a few minutes' walk from one of the city's least-expensive full-service hotels. Located near Phrom Phong Skytrain station, the rooms come with refrigerator, satellite television and bathrooms with hairdryers. There's an outdoor swimming pool. The Splash Coffeeshop is open all day. 209 rooms.

The Peninsula $$$$ *333 Charoen Nakhon Road, Khlong San, Bangkok 10600, tel: 0 2861 2888, fax: 0 2861 1112, <www.penin sula.com>*. With every room facing the river, this 39-storey luxury hotel is the city's most modern. Rooms come with silent fax machines and marble bathrooms with steam-free TVs. There's an outdoor pool, a health club, three excellent restaurants and an elegant lobby bar. Free shuttle boats to Tha Sathorn pier. 370 rooms.

Plaza Athénée $$$ *Wireless Road, Bangkok 10330, tel: 0 2650 8800, fax: 0 2650 8500, <www.starwoodhotels.com>.* One of the city's newest luxury hotels caters to business travellers. Situated near the US Embassy, it has quick access to the express road to the airport. A tall, shiny glass building houses spacious rooms with marble bathrooms. A small but attractive outdoor pool surrounds an exercise room and a spa. Smooth Curry serves traditional Thai food while The Rain Tree Café offers international cuisines. 378 rooms.

Rembrandt Hotel $$ *19 Sukhumvit Soi 18, Klong Toei, Bangkok 10110, tel: 0 2261 7100, fax: 0 2261 7017, <www.rembrandtbkk. com>.* A large, newer first-class hotel popular with European tour operators, in the heart of the city's commercial centre. Rooms are spacious and well-equipped with mini-bars, safes, bathrobes and hairdryers. There are three restaurants serving Mexican, Indian and Thai cuisine, plus a pool and fitness centre. 407 rooms.

Shangri-La $$$ *89 Soi Wat Suan Plu, New Road, Bangrak, Bangkok 10500, tel: 0 2236 7777, fax: 0 2236 8579, <www. shangri-la.com>.* An oasis of luxury in the heart of the city, facing the Chao Phraya River. Expect deluxe rooms with every amenity, although bathrooms are a bit small. There is a lovely pool set amid a lush tropical garden, while an attractive riverside restaurant serves delicate Thai cuisine and a new holistic spa has therapies inspired by traditional Chinese healing systems. English tea is served at the grand open lobby. 850 rooms.

The Swiss Lodge $$ *3 Convent Road, Silom, Bangkok 10500, tel: 0 2233 5345, fax: 0 2236 9425, <www.swisslodge.com>.* A small boutique hotel located near the nightlife and shopping districts, and the Saladaeng Skytrain station. Swiss-managed with friendly, knowledgeable staff. Elegant rooms with teak furniture and marble bathrooms. There's 24-hour room service, a small pool with sundeck and a Swiss café. 46 rooms.

CHIANG MAI

Chiang Mai Plaza Hotel $ *92 Si Donchai Road, Amphoe Muang, 50100, tel: 0 5390 3161, fax: 0 5327 9457, <www.cnxplaza.com>.* Within walking distance of the Night Bazaar and the Ping River, this large tourist hotel offers great value. Its spacious public areas are tastefully decorated with Thai art and maintain a relaxed ambience. In the evenings a small Northern Thai music ensemble performs in the main lobby. Facilities include a fitness centre, large outdoor pool and two restaurants serving Thai and international cuisine. 467 rooms, 8 suites.

The Four Seasons Resort Chiang Mai $$$$ *Mae Rim-Samoeng Old Road, Mae Rim, 50180, tel: 0 5329 8181, fax: 0 5329 8190, <www.fourseasons.com/chiangmai>.* Thirty minutes from the airport, this world-renowned, lushly landscaped resort hotel overlooks tranquil rice paddies. Accommodation is in two-storey teak pavilions luxuriously furnished with every amenity, including CD players and huge bathrooms with deep tubs. These also come with private *sala* (a traditional-style covered verandah) with an oversized day bed and colourful Thai pillows. There's an infinity pool, tennis courts, a spa, a fitness centre and two outstanding restaurants. Shuttle service to the night bazaar is provided daily. 64 suites; 16 residences.

Sheraton Chiangmai $$ *318/1 Chiangmai-Lumphun Road, Amphoe Muang, 50000, tel: 0 5327 5300, fax: 0 5327 5299, <www.sheraton-chiangmai.com>.* The most luxurious hotel within the city centre, a 10-minute drive from the night bazaar. Expect spacious rooms with deluxe amenities; bathrooms have separate bath/shower. There's a small outdoor pool with a bar, an exercise room, a spa offering Thai massage and two restaurants. 526 rooms.

CHIANG RAI

Dusit Island Resort $$ *1129 Kraisorasit Road, Vieng District, 57000, tel: 0 5371 5777, fax: 0 5371 5801, <chiangrai.dusit.com>.* An excellent hotel located on an island in the Kok river, across from the city centre. Rooms have large picture windows overlooking the city and mountains. There's a large outdoor pool, tennis courts, fitness centre, a steak house, a Chinese restaurant, a Thai café and an English pub. 271 rooms.

CHIANG SAEN/THE GOLDEN TRIANGLE

Anantara Resort and Spa Golden Triangle $$ 229 Moo 1, Wiang, *Chiang Saen, 57150, tel: 0 5378 4084, fax: 0 5378 4090, <www.anantara.com>*. A most unusual low-rise hotel (two-storey buildings) set amid 81 hectares (200 acres) of manicured gardens. The spacious and comfortable rooms with sunken bathrooms all come with a large terrace overlooking the Mekong River, Myanmar and Laos. A recently established elephant camp offers local elephant treks and mahout lessons. 103 rooms.

MAE HONG SON

Imperial Tara Mae Hong Son $ 149 Moo 8, Pang Moo, Muang, *58000, tel: 0 5368 4449, fax: 0 5368 4440, <www.imperialhotels. com>*. A 15-minute walk from the centre of town, this first-class hotel overlooks a teak forest. The large rooms all come with gleaming teak floors and private balconies with views of the forest or the lovely kidney-shaped pool. There's a beautiful terrace where meals are served in the dry season. 104 rooms.

PHUKET

Amanpuri $$$$ *Pansea Beach, 83000, tel: 0 7632 4333, fax: 0 7632 4100, <www.amanpuri.com>*. The premier property of the exclusive Amanresorts chain has a private beach where every imaginable water sport is available. Perfect for the many movie stars who arrive each year. Pavilions with wood floors and ocean views are scattered on the hillside amid coconut and palm trees. There's also a beautiful pool and the hotel has its own fleet of yachts for day trips or overnight cruises. 40 pavilions; 30 private villas.

Banyan Tree $$$$ *33 Moo 4 Srisoonthorn Road, Amphoe Talang, 83110, tel: 0 7632 4374, fax: 0 7632 4375, <www.banyantree.com>*.

The epitome of luxury in the midst of a manicured development at Bang Tao Bay. All the villas have wood floors, plush furniture and private outdoor Jacuzzis; some even come with private pools, although few overlook the sea. There are free-form and lap pools, tennis courts, water sports, a spa and fitness centre and three outstanding restaurants. 108 villas.

Marina Phuket Resort $$ *47 Karon Road, Karon Beach, 83100, tel: 0 7633 0625, fax: 0 7633 0516, <www.marinaphuket.com>.* Small, simply furnished bungalows are scattered on a hillside a few minutes' walk from the sandy beach at Karon. The jungle-like foliage means some rooms remain quite dark throughout the day; the sea view units have breathtaking views. There are two restaurants and a small pool. 104 rooms.

Plub Pla Resort $$$ *137/6–7 Patak Road, Karon, 83100, tel: 0 7628 5167, fax: 0 7628 5170, <www.plubpla.com>.* An unusual and elegant mountain-top retreat located in the midst of lush gardens with panoramic views of the island. The six exquisite rooms all have teak floors and minimal furniture, creating a pleasant Zen-like atmosphere. Every room has a large terrace with spectacular views. There's a pool and two outstanding restaurants. 6 rooms.

Le Royal Méridien Phuket Yacht Club $$$$ *Nai Harn Beach, 83100, tel: 0 7638 0200, fax: 0 7638 0280, <www.starwood hotels.com>.* A lovely hideaway on a cliff above a white-sand beach. Understated luxury in well-equipped rooms that feature oversized terraces with magnificent ocean views. The spa has outdoor treatment rooms overlooking the Andaman Sea and there's a pool, three restaurants and an exercise room. 110 rooms.

Thavorn Beach Village and Spa $$ *6/2 Moo 6, Nakalay Bay, Patong, 83150, tel: 0 7629 0334, fax: 0 7634 0384, <www.thavorn beachvillage.com>.* Close to the bustle of Patong, yet tranquil enough with its own private beach. A cable car transports guests from the open-air main lobby to the comfortable rooms built high on a hill. The grounds are lush and service is of high standards. There's a large pool, a new spa and an excellent Thai restaurant. 194 rooms.

KO SAMUI

Central Samui Beach Resort $$ 38/2 Moo 3, Bo Phut, *Chaweng Beach, 84320, tel: 0 7723 0500, fax: 0 7742 2385, <www.centralhotelsresorts.com>.* This is the largest resort hotel in the midst of bustling Chaweng Beach. Rooms are comfortable with their own little private balconies, all with ocean views. There's a fitness centre, spa and three excellent restaurants. 208 rooms.

The Imperial Boat House Hotel $$ *83 Moo 5, Choeng Mon Beach, 84320, tel: 0 7742 5041, fax: 0 7742 5460, <www.imperial hotels.com/boathouse>.* This splendid property features 210 comfortable hotel rooms, including 34 rice barge suites with wood floors, luxury bathrooms and amenities. Public areas feature a pool and a beachside restaurant.

Poppies Samui $$$ *Chaweng Beach, 84320, tel: 0 7742 2419, fax: 0 7742 2420 <www.poppiessamui.com>.* Excellent location at the quieter end of Chaweng Beach; a small property with understated luxury in each of its private cottages decorated with fine Thai silk and gleaming teak floors and furniture. The bathrooms feature a sunken bath opening onto a private garden. There's a pool surrounded with natural rock, an outstanding restaurant on the beach and a spa. 24 cottages.

Le Royal Méridien Baan Taling Ngam $$$$ *295 Moo 3, Taling Ngam Beach, 84140, tel: 0 7742 9100, fax: 0 7742 3220, <www.starwoodhotels.com>.* An hour's drive from Chaweng and the airport, this exclusive hideaway offers a luxurious beach holiday. The spacious rooms and villas all come with teak furniture and most offer panoramic views out to sea and to the islands of Ang Thong Marine National Park. Luxury amenities include DVD and CD players. There's a variety of water sports, seven swimming pools, a spa and three restaurants. 70 rooms.

Santiburi Resort $$$$ *12/12 Moo 1, Mae Nam, 84330, tel: 0 7742 5031, fax: 0 7742 5040, <www.santiburi.com>.* This 9-hectare (23-acre) luxury resort prides itself on its quiet, restful atmosphere.

There's a lovely stretch of private sandy beach with every water sport imaginable. Accommodation is in villas scattered across the grounds, all meticulously decorated with an authentic flair. There's a new spa, a glorious pool and three restaurants. 59 Thai-style villas; 12 suites.

The Tongsai Bay $$$$ *84 Moo 5, Bophut, Tongsai Bay, 84320, tel: 0 7724 5480, fax: 0 7742 5462, <www.tongsaibay.co.th>.* On a quiet bay with a private beach, this hideaway is one of the most luxuriously unpretentious retreats in Thailand. The cottages, scattered on a hillside, all have teak floors, open-air terraces and secluded outdoor tubs. The villas have indoor and outdoor bedrooms (mosquito nets provided), an unusual feature for an airy tropical vacation. 44 cottages, 24 beachfront suites, 15 villas.

HUA HIN

Evason Hua Hin Resort and Spa $$$ *9 Parknampran Beach, Prachuab Khiri Khan, 77220, tel: 0 3263 2111, fax: 0 3263 2112, <www.six-senses.com/evason-huahin>.* Modern elegance along an isolated beach with the option of private pool villas. The Six Senses Spa offers a range of treatments. 145 rooms, 40 villas.

KRABI BEACHES

Rayavadee $$$ *214 Moo 2, Tambon Aonang Amphoe Muang, tel: 0 7562 0740, fax: 0 7562 0630, <www.rayavadee.com>.* Idyllic two-storey pavilions set in coconut groves next to huge cliffs and bordering three beaches. Full range of restaurants, bars, tennis, spa and water sports. 77 rooms.

KO PHI PHI

Holiday Inn Resort Phi Phi Island $–$$ *54 Moo 8, Tambon Aonang Koh Phi Phi, 83000, tel: 0 7562 7300, fax: 08 1476 3787, <www.phiphi-palmbeach.com>.* Depending on the season, this smart resort goes from mid- to high-range in price, due to its location at the remote northerly end of the island. Its isolation means tranquillity, though sightseeing is best accomplished by boat. 77 bungalows.

Recommended Restaurants

There is no shortage of restaurants in Thailand, from streetside eateries to award-winning establishments in spectacular settings. In Bangkok, restaurants within the deluxe hotels still reign as the crème de la crème of the city's best. The good news is that even a grand meal in a top hotel is considerably more affordable than the price of a similar meal in other large capitals, such as London or New York. Service at most restaurants is usually superb.

Most restaurants accept credit cards but streetside eateries do not. Reservations are essential only at the most expensive establishments in Bangkok, and usually for dinner only. In Phuket and Ko Samui it's advisable that you call a day or two ahead for dinner reservations during the high season from December to March.

Many restaurants do not open for breakfast. Lunch is usually served from noon to 3pm and dinner from 6.30 to 10pm. In Bangkok and the north it's quite common that the last order for dinner be taken around 9.30pm, especially on weekday evenings. At the resorts, restaurants usually serve until 11pm.

The following prices are for a three-course meal, excluding drinks and tips. Also note that more expensive items – such as lobster or salmon – will substantially increase the bill. Wine in Thailand is prohibitively expensive due to the import tax.

$$$$	over US$25
$$$	US$15–25
$$	US$5–15
$	less than US$5

BANGKOK

Anna's Café $ *118 Soi Saladaeng, Silom, tel: 0 2632 0619.* Open daily 11am–10pm. The first of several branches in Bangkok, this famous café is popular with a younger crowd as it's laid back enough for just a light snack with a glass of wine or a large salad. The main dishes are good too, including smoked catfish and vegetarian curry. Desserts and coffee drinks are a major draw.

Baan Khanitha $$$ *69 Sathorn Tai Road, tel: 0 2675 4200.* Open daily for lunch and dinner. This long-established restaurant recently moved to a new location but is still highly popular among Western expats and tourists for its toned-down yet tasty Thai cuisine. Specialities include grilled cottonfish wrapped in a banana leaf and delicately prepared cashew-pineapple rice, served in a pineapple. For dessert, there's mango with sticky rice.

Biscotti $$$ *Four Seasons Hotel, 155 Ratchadamri Road, tel: 0 2255 5443.* Open daily for breakfast, lunch and dinner. One of the most popular Italian restaurants in Bangkok is casual but elegant with a contemporary flair and an open kitchen. There's a wood-fired oven for the inventive pizzas (such as the lobster tail pizza with forest mushrooms) and the fragrant *focaccia* bread with herbs. Risottos, pastas and a few meat dishes round out the short menu.

Celadon $$$$ *The Sukhothai, 13/3 South Sathorn Road, tel: 0 2287 0222.* Open daily for lunch and dinner. Wonderfully located in the Zen-like Sukhothai hotel, overlooking a lotus pond. Here you can sample true Royal Thai cuisine served by very knowledgeable staff who can help you combine dishes to create a most memorable meal. Banana blossom salad, spicy kingfish soup and sweet-and-sour tofu are just a few of the specialities. Desserts are outstanding.

The China House $$$$ *just outside the Oriental hotel, 48 Oriental Avenue, tel: 0 2236 0400.* Open daily for lunch and dinner. The best and most formal Chinese restaurant in the city is located in a beautiful colonial style house. Specialities include such hard-to-find delicacies as double-boiled shark's fin soup, marinated octopus with preserved duck egg, and braised sea cucumber with garlic. Dim sum is available for lunch only. Service is superb.

Le Dalat $$ *47/1 Sukhumvit Soi 23, tel: 0 2258 4192.* Open daily for lunch and dinner. Long established as the leading Vietnamese restaurant in the city. Bright and airy and always busy, Le Dalat's specialities include Vietnamese spring rolls made with fresh vegetables and herbs, fried squid and beef simmered with mint leaves.

Harmonique $$ *22 Charoenkrung Soi 34, tel: 0 2237 8175.* Open Monday to Saturday for lunch and dinner. One of the most unusual eateries in Bangkok is hidden in a secret garden near the French Embassy. The home-cooked Thai food is carefully prepared and presented. The traditional soup is served in clay pots and the curried fish is exquisite. There's a small wine list.

Kalpapruek on First $ *The Emporium, 1st floor, 662 Sukhumvit Soi 24, tel: 0 2664 8410.* Open daily for lunch and dinner. This airy restaurant located within Bangkok's most elegant shopping centre is popular with local professionals and serves consistently good (and very affordable) Asian food. The dishes include a mix of Thai, Chinese and Indian ingredients such as curries served with *roti* and Chinese sausage.

Kuppa Cafe and Restaurant $$$ *39 Sukhumvit Soi 16, tel: 0 2663 0450.* Open daily for breakfast, lunch and dinner. Come here if you want to dine with Bangkok's hip crowd. Thoroughly modern in design with lots of glass and metal, this restaurant serves both Thai and Western specialities, including a large array of vegetarian dishes. The Australian owners change the menu often and use local ingredients to create a fusion of tastes. Good selection of affordable Australian wines.

Mango Tree $$$ *37 Soi Tantawan, Surawongse, tel: 0 2236 2820.* Open daily for lunch and dinner. This lovely Thai restaurant is housed within a charming old house offering indoor/outdoor dining just steps from the busy Patpong neighbourhood. Specialities include fresh and spicy mango salad, chicken baked in pandanus leaf and a variety of green curries. There's Thai dancing on weekend evenings.

New York Steakhouse $$$$ *JW Marriott Hotel, 4 Sukhumvit Soi 2, tel: 0 2656 7700.* Open daily for dinner. A pleasant and very contemporary restaurant serving the best steaks in the city. Aged to perfection, grain-fed Angus beef is flown in from the US along with excellent (and more affordable) Australian steaks. There's also a large selection of seafood including fresh lobster, swordfish and salmon. There's an extensive wine list – and martinis with olives, of course.

Salathip $$$$ *Shangri-La hotel, 89 Soi Wat Suan Phu, tel: 0 2236 7777.* Open daily for dinner. In a romantic setting on the banks of the river, this Thai restaurant has been consistently rated one of the best in the city. Dishes include delicate specialities such as pomelo salad with grilled prawn and roasted duck flavoured with curry and coconut milk. Desserts include the traditional flour balls with coconut milk and jackfruit.

Supatra River House $$ *226 Soi Wat Rakhang, Arun Amarin Road, tel: 0 2411 0305.* Open daily for lunch and dinner. This old two-storey riverside house offers excellent Thai food in a stylish and elegant setting, with views of Wat Phra Kaew and Wat Arun. Dinner on Fridays and Saturdays can be followed by a Thai classical dance performance at the affiliated Patravadi Theatre nearby. There is a free ferry service from the Maharaj Pier.

CHIANG MAI

The Gallery $$ *25–29 Charoenrat Road, tel: 0 5324 8601.* Open daily from noon–midnight. This lovely restaurant is located on the banks of the River Ping in an old teakwood house that doubles as an art gallery. There's a wide variety of northern Thai dishes as well as a good selection of vegetarian specialities and a small wine list.

Nang Nual Seafood Restaurant $$ *27 Ko Klang Road, tel: 0 5328 1974.* Open daily from 8am–10.30pm. A few minutes outside the city centre, this large riverside restaurant is shaded by teakwood trees and offers an enormous selection of fresh seafood. There are aquariums filled with live lobsters and crabs. Other specialities include roasted pork with sugarcane and grilled river prawns.

PHUKET

Baan Rim Pa $$$$ *100/7 Kalim Beach Road, Patong, tel: 0 7634 0789.* Open daily for lunch and dinner. One of the best restaurants in Thailand sits on a cliff overlooking the ocean. Exquisitely prepared Thai food includes such specialities as steamed fish in pickled-plum sauce and hot-and-sour soup with fish and vegetables. Good selection of vegetarian dishes.

The Boathouse Wine & Grill $$$ *Mom Tri's Boathouse, 12 Kata Noi Road, Kata Beach, tel: 0 7633 0015.* Open daily from 7.30am–11.30pm. Offering fine views of the Andaman Sea, this beach-front restaurant features refined Thai and European dining as well as seafood specialties. There is also a large wine selection. Indoor and outdoor seating available.

Tamarind Spa Restaurant $$ *Banyan Tree Phuket, tel: 0 7632 4374.* Open daily for lunch and dinner. This cool, airy and shaded restaurant is located alongside the serene and Zen-like lap pool at a luxurious resort hotel. The unusual (but very affordable) menu features low-calorie specialities such as soba-noodle salad with fresh greens, vegetable juice cocktails and delicious sandwiches. Only the freshest market ingredients are used, along with local herbs and spices, to add a subtle fusion of Thai flavours to every dish.

KO SAMUI

Betelnut $$$ *46/27 Chaweng Boulevard, tel: 0 7741 3370.* Open daily from 6.30pm–11pm. Celebrated chef Jeffrey Lord has opened this small elegant restaurant on a side-street behind the Central Samui Hotel. He uses only the freshest local ingredients to create a fusion of Californian and Thai cuisine. Specialities include crispy soft-shell crab, sea scallops with Pernod cream and salmon with a tamarind glaze. The homemade desserts are exquisite.

Ko-Seng $ *95/1 Moo, Maenam Beach, tel: 0 7742 5365.* Open daily 10am–10pm. Excellent Thai food in a very simple, family-run dining room. Specialities include several different types of Thai curry. The coconut fish is delicious. For something different, try the fresh crab with curry and chilli sauce or the Thai soup with coconut chicken. No credit cards.

Poppies Restaurant $$$ *Poppies Samui resort, Chaweng Beach, tel: 0 7742 2419.* Open daily for breakfast, lunch and dinner. One of the most romantic restaurant on the island is right on the beach and serves Thai cuisine infused with a Western twist such as the popular prawn cakes with plum sauce and charcoal roasted duck. There's also an excellent selection of fusion dishes such as the chicken filled with crabmeat and baked in a seafood sauce.

CHIANG RAI

Cabbages and Condoms $$ *620/26 Thanalai Road, tel: 0 5371 9167.* Sister of the ever popular C+C in Bangkok, this restaurant is tied to the social cause of population control. Great Thai cuisine.

MAE HONG SON

Fern Restaurant $ *87 Khunlumpraphat Road, tel: 0 5361 1374.* This rustic restaurant near Jong Kum Lake is one of the town's best. The typically spicy dishes are cooked with a deft touch and are not too overpowering.

HUA HIN

Baan Thalia $$–$$$ *Anantara Resort and Spa, 43/1 Phet Kasem Road, tel: 0 3252 0250.* Local arts and crafts line the walls of this elegant contemporary Italian restaurant, which has an exceptionally creative menu blending Thai and Italian influences.

KRABI BEACHES

Krua Phranang $$$ *Rayavadee Resort, Phra Nang Beach, tel: 0 7562 0740/3.* Al fresco Thai restaurant on Krabi's best beach, which offers wonderful views of the sunset beyond the scattered islands and great seafood, including barbecue classics.

INDEX

Berlitz® Pocket Guide

Thailand

Fourth Edition 2008

Written by Ben Davies
Updated by Joe Cummings
Series Editor: Tony Halliday

Photography credits
Jon Davison 1, 6, 10, 14, 18, 36, 39, 43, 53, 57, 59, 60, 61, 62, 64, 69, 76, 87, 93, 94; Francis Dorai/APA 25; David Henley/CPA 38, 47, 48 Luca Invernizzi Tettoni 16; Jason Lang 52; Marcus Wilson-Smith 7, 8, 11, 12, 13, 17, 20, 24, 25, 27, 29, 30, 32, 33, 34, 40, 41, 44, 49, 50, 54, 63, 66, 70, 71, 72, 75, 79, 80, 82, 84, 88, 90, 92, 96, 98, 101, 102, 103, 104

Cover picture: Walter Bibikow/Jon Arnold Images

All Rights Reserved
© 2008 Berlitz Publishing/Apa Publications GmbH & Co. Verlag KG, Singapore Branch, Singapore

Printed in Singapore by Insight Print Services (Pte) Ltd, 38 Joo Koon Road, Singapore 628990. Tel: (65) 6865-1600. Fax: (65) 6861-6438

Berlitz Trademark Reg. U.S. Patent Office and other countries. Marca Registrada

Every effort has been made to provide accurate information in this publication, but changes are inevitable. The publisher cannot be responsible for any resulting loss, inconvenience or injury.

Contact us

At Berlitz we strive to keep our guides as accurate and up to date as possible, but if you find anything that has changed, or if you have any suggestions on ways to improve this guide, then we would be delighted to hear from you.

Berlitz Publishing, PO Box 7910,
London SE1 1WE, England
fax: (44) 20 7403 0290
email: berlitz@apaguide.co.uk
www.berlitzpublishing.com